Unbelievable Crimes Volume Five

Unbelievable Crimes, Volume 5

Daniela Airlie

Published by Daniela Airlie, 2023.

While every precaution has been taken in the preparation of this book, the publisher assumes no responsibility for errors or omissions, or for damages resulting from the use of the information contained herein.

UNBELIEVABLE CRIMES VOLUME FIVE

First edition. August 10, 2023.

Copyright © 2023 Daniela Airlie.

Written by Daniela Airlie.

Table of Contents

Unbelievable Crimes Volume Five 1

Prologue 3

Deadly Obsession 5

Dying To Be Popular 19

Bound By Heartlessness 37

Murderous Matriarch 59

The Girl With Grit 71

Hunger For Depravity 83

Evil Among Us 91

She Killed To See What It Felt Like 101

Better Late Than Never 107

Final Thoughts 117

The right of Daniela Airlie as the publisher and owner of this work has been asserted in accordance with the Copyright, Designs, and Patents Act 1988. No part of this publication may be reproduced in any format without the publisher's prior written consent. This book is for entertainment and informational purposes only.

Although research from various sources has gone into this book, neither the author nor publisher will be held responsible for any inaccuracies. To the best of the knowledge of the author, all information within this publication is factually correct, derived from researching these cases thoroughly. The author may offer speculation and/or opinion about the cases covered throughout this book.

Danielaairlie.carrd.co[1]

---

1. http://danielaairlie.carrd.co

Prologue

Welcome to the fifth installment of the *Unbelievable Crimes* series.

Consuming the amount of true crime content that I do - I read countless crime books, watch old episodes of true crime shows, and listen to several podcasts dedicated to the topic - I'm surprised at my ability to still find cases that shock me. The fact that I still get upset and frustrated by true crime is a good sign, I suppose. I'm not hardened to it; I still have copious amounts of empathy and, most of all, a strong desire for justice to be served.

I've noticed that's a theme among us true crime followers: we all have a super strong sense of justice. While we may read about cold cases and unsolved murders, they leave us feeling empty and disappointed that the culprit could get away with their horrific acts. You may be relieved to hear that this book has none of these cases included.

True crime followers like justice served cold - slapped in the criminal's face as hard as possible - ensuring the culprit knows the crimes they committed were abhorrent. We get a strong sense of satisfaction knowing a violent offender is off the streets and securely segregated from good citizens with kind intentions.

Part of the reason we consume true crime is to see justice served well, although you may agree that no prison sentence will ever dampen the pain and heartache the criminal caused through their violent actions. Still, for them to be made to face up to their crimes publicly, for their names forever to be tarnished, and for their freedom to be stripped away is a much better scenario than the criminal being free and roaming the streets.

In this anthology, I'll take you through some truly heinous crimes committed by equally heinous individuals. From murderous mothers to killer kids, there's no escaping the stark reality that some people are just plain wicked.

As always, bear in mind these tales are true and are somebody's reality. They contain details of real-life violence and descriptions of horrific assaults.

With that said, if you're ready, let's begin.

Deadly Obsession

In the U.K., someone is reported missing every minute and a half. Oftentimes, these people are found pretty quickly. They've perhaps needed a break from the stresses of the people around them, taken themselves off in a drunken haze, or fled an abusive situation and taken shelter away from their tormentor.

In some instances, though, these missing people never turn up. Some are discovered dead, either at their own hands or someone else's. Other times, the missing individual is neither found dead nor alive. Sadly, the case I'm about to cover is the latter, but it's not a cold case - and we know how frustrating those are. The killer was captured despite 15-year-old Danielle Jones' body never being found, a rarity in true crime cases.

Danielle was a shy, naive teenager who her family adored. She was close with her mother, Linda, and her father, Tony. The teen was never in trouble and, despite being 15, hadn't developed a rebellious streak. She never talked back to her mother, was keen to abide by her parent's rules, and didn't dare step out of line for fear of upsetting her mother.

Those close to the teen would describe her as quite timid, although once you got to know her, she'd reveal her funny, playful side that was reserved for the few she trusted. Danielle was the last person you'd imagine bunking off school, so when Linda Jones got a call on the afternoon of June 18, 2001, advising her that Danielle hadn't turned up for class, she had no idea what to think.

After considering the options, Linda presumed her daughter must have decided to skip school that day. After all, she'd watched her walk to the bus stop that morning, a short journey that was five minutes from her home. The morning routine for Danielle was always the same: get up, get dressed, have breakfast, make two sandwiches for lunch, pack them neatly in her lunchbox, and head out the door just before 9 am to catch the school bus.

In the three years she'd been in high school, she'd always hopped on the bus and made it to school, never once bunking off. She'd never even missed the bus before. She always arrived at school on time and arrived home at the same time. The teenager was a creature of habit, so the idea she'd decided to flout the rules was almost unfathomable for Linda. However, the mother couldn't comprehend the alternative - that she'd been abducted.

The Jones' lived in Stanford le Hope, a small town in Essex. Surrounded by nature reserves, the little city has a village-like feel, with old-style pubs, centuries-old buildings, and churches lining the city center streets. The idea that their daughter could have been taken in broad daylight just didn't seem plausible. The streets were bustling with schoolchildren at the time Danielle left the house, so if something had happened, surely they would have seen it and spoken up about it.

Linda sat all afternoon and waited for Danielle to come through the front door. She was preparing for her daughter to give her a tall tale about why she couldn't attend school. *This is Danielle acting out, finally developing a rebellious side*, her mother thought. The hours rolled by slowly; 6 pm came, and there was no sign of the girl. Soon, it would be night time, and Danielle was scared of the dark, so they were sure she'd walk through the door, excuses in tow. If she didn't, they'd have to consider the terrifying alternative.

The painstaking hours passing by gave Linda time to ruminate on her daughter's life up until that point.

Danielle was her only daughter. She'd been a cute, happy baby, full of smiles for her parents. Growing up, she was somewhat of a tomboy, being the elder sister to two younger brothers whom she doted on. She adored animals and was full of compassion for all creatures. As she developed into her teens, she became painfully aware of her looks, something that got the sensitive girl down. As most young girls do, she'd compare herself to her peers unfavorably. Her mother would offer her reassurance, but of course, the young girl did not heed Linda's words of comfort.

Boys - or any kind of young love - hadn't been a part of Danielle's life thus far. She was only 15, but some of her friends had already gotten into youthful relationships. Linda would recall her daughter being very private and shy when it came to what she wore and how she presented herself. This reminded Linda of a time when the family was on holiday, and she took a picture of her three children enjoying the sun. In the photo, Danielle had a black vest on. Modest, as she always was, but her collarbones were exposed. When the photograph was shown to Danielle's uncle, Stuart Campbell, he made some strange comments. He suggested that he could see Danielle's breasts in the innocent shot.

The more Linda thought about it, the more she pieced together a number of interactions she found strange between Danielle and Stuart. As she entered her teens, Stuart showed much more interest in his young niece. He would meet her as she got off the school bus and convince her to jump in his work van and run errands with him. He seemed to want to spend quite a lot of time with the girl. Stuart didn't offer the same attention to his young nephews, however.n one.

As darkness hit, Linda and the rest of the family decided to head out and trawl the streets to see if they could find Danielle. They hoped she was merely too afraid to go home after bunking off school for the day, but they knew deep down something more sinister was at play. Numerous laps of the local estates found nothing. Linda headed home to wait for Danielle in case she turned up, while dad Tony headed to his brother's house to see if he'd heard anything. The worried father noted that Stuart was the only member of the family who hadn't been wandering the streets to look for Danielle. It angered him, although he didn't raise the issue with his brother. He had bigger things to worry about. But, still, why wasn't he helping search for the niece he seemingly doted on?

The following day, the police arrived at the Joneses. The family no doubt had endured a sleepless night waiting for Danielle, their minds conjuring up all the horrific scenarios in which the teen may have found herself.

Officers informed the family they were going to use sniffer dogs to see if they could retrace the girl's last steps, which the clever dogs did successfully - up to a certain point. Danielle had walked her usual route, the dogs confirmed this, but then the trail stopped suddenly. It seemed she'd either vanished into thin air or got into a vehicle, one that most certainly wasn't the school bus.

The Joneses felt a tidal wave of relief when Stuart visited them to let them know Danielle had texted him to tell him she was in "so much trouble." *Yes, she was*, Linda thought, but she couldn't wait for the teenager to walk through the door. According to Stuart, Danielle told him to tell her mum that she was sorry and thanked him for being so nice to her. She called him the "best uncle ever." The message gave the family hope the teen was safe, but the hunt was still on to find her.

Police knocked on hundreds of houses in the area and asked residents to check their outdoor areas and sheds to see if the missing girl was there. Nothing came up. Days passed, and there was no sign of Danielle. As you may know, the first 72 hours when searching for a missing person are critical. Those three days had passed, and hope was waning despite the messages from Danielle apologizing for running away.

Danielle's school friends talked among themselves. They agreed it was most unlike the girl to just take off. She never put a foot out of line. They also agreed that her relationship with her uncle Stuart was weird. Danielle had told them that he'd taken her to the cinema and held her hand.

The friends never told an adult about this disturbing revelation since they didn't want to get anyone into trouble. The teens perhaps didn't see it this way at the time, but Stuart was grooming his niece. All they knew was that he gave Danielle lots of attention, and sometimes this would stress her out. His constant texting, his blatant upset if Danielle declined an invitation to go somewhere, and his persistent pet names for her were all picked up on. They hadn't considered that there was more to this inappropriate relationship than met the eye.

Stuart's newfound interest in his relative saw the man, who was three decades older than Danielle, try to cause tension between the girl and her parents. He'd create false issues and present them to Danielle, telling her that he wouldn't put up with the way her parents treated her. *Don't let them boss you around, you're your own person. Don't let them speak to you like that; respect is a two-way street.*

He would then run back to Linda and Tony and advise them that Danielle's teenage attitude was something they needed to keep in check. *The way she speaks to you is shocking - she needs to be kept in line. Start demanding respect from her.*

None of them realized he was playing a sneaky game, trying to segregate the teen from her caregivers. To an extent, it worked. Stuart had become the comforting presence in Danielle's life and inserted himself directly between the mother and daughter.

With the days quickly passing and no movement in the case, the papers were picking up on the story, and Linda and Tony held a press conference, begging their girl to come home. They also tried to appeal to her possible kidnappers' human side and pleaded for them to set her free. Danielle's school photo was now being circulated, enabling more people to come to know her face should they see her in the area.

Meanwhile, the police were seeking out any witnesses on the morning of Danielle's disappearance. They also took an interest in Stuart Campbell and carried out a background check on him. What they found would be troubling.

Just the year prior, he'd abducted a 14-year-old girl. His sentence was light considering the charge: he didn't do any time behind bars. If he had, you might consider that I wouldn't be writing this chapter you're reading now.

It was a startling revelation, and it put him directly in the center of the police's radar. A further look into him found he was a known predator, with multiple young girls falling victim to his perversions. It was also discovered that Stuart moonlighted as a photographer. His regular job was as a builder, but in his free time, he'd take pictures in his "home studio." However, the only people he seemed to take photos of were young girls, often around the age of 13. He'd lure the girls to his studio - a description of his set-up that you should take lightly - by promising them modeling gigs.

This side hustle was known to Stuart's family, but they weren't aware of the subjects of his photos. At one point, he was brought in for police questioning over his suspicious business, but no further action was seemingly taken. He brushed it off to family, saying one of the girls he'd been taking pictures of had been requesting him to take inappropriate snaps, and his refusal angered her, so she called the police. It seemed like his family believed him at the time.

The investigators dealing with Danielle's disappearance were scoping Stuart. They were hesitant to arrest him, though, concerned that if Danielle was still alive, they might ruin her chances of making out of her ordeal alive. Only he knew where she was, and if they removed him from the equation too soon, it might result in the teenager's demise. It was too risky for now.

So, they watched his every move, hoping he'd lead them right back to the girl. They found his behavior to be quite strange. He was driving around, seemingly aimlessly, stopping at parking lot after parking lot. Eventually, police noticed a pattern: in each parking area, he was finding silver cars and taking pictures of them. A far cry from the teenage girls he often snapped - with or without their consent - but still a strange thing to do.

It dawned on police that the cars Stuart was photographing all resembled his own silver car. When the suspect didn't lead officers to the girl, it was decided they'd bite the bullet and arrest him. They pinned all their hopes on an intense interrogation of the man. Stuart was cool and collected under questioning - until the heavy questions began, that is.

Investigators asked Stuart what it was about 15-year-old Danielle that he liked so much. Why he wanted to be with the youngster so much. Eventually, he began to give "no comment" answers as it became apparent the police were onto him.

Tony Jones was given the news his brother had been brought in for questioning over Danielle's disappearance. The Joneses were already dealing with the dizzying, nauseating idea that their only daughter had been murdered, but to think it was at the hands of a family member was too much to comprehend. Surely he'd have a solid alibi, or CCTV of where he was at the time of Danielle's vanishing - that would firmly clear his name.

It came as something of a relief when Stuart was released without charge since there was no tangible evidence to tie him to the girl's disappearance. After all, all the police knew at this point was Stuart was smug, behaving strangely, and had a predilection for young girls. No rock solid evidence.

Stuart's arrest caused the Joneses to look retrospectively at the way he was around their daughter. They searched her bedroom and found notes Stuart had written his niece, in which he called her "flower." A once seemingly innocent term of endearment suddenly became sinister for the heartbroken parents. Why would Stuart leave her notes? Why not just talk to her in front of the rest of the family?

This caused the parents to agree that Stuart often took Danielle to one side for quiet conversations where nobody else could hear. At the time, this didn't cause any alarm. Now, though, the parents were realizing Stuart may have been grooming Danielle all along. The girl was notoriously quiet and wouldn't have spoken up for fear of getting her uncle into trouble.

The police obtained a warrant to search Stuart's property. From the evidence they'd gathered so far, they felt Stuart had initiated an inappropriate relationship with Danielle. They just needed some proof. They'd also gained some new intel after Stuart's release from interrogation. A witness spotted Danielle chatting to a man who fitted Stuart's description the morning she vanished. The man was driving a blue van, just like Stuart's work vehicle. All of these small pieces of evidence were coming together and pointing straight toward Stuart Campbell.

Investigators searched his property with a fine-tooth comb. They found nothing - until they made their way to his attic. Here, he'd hidden a green bag that had some disturbing items flung into it: women's underwear, Danielle's used lip gloss, and white blood-stained hosiery stockings.

The evidence was sent away for testing. Meanwhile, Stuart's phone records showed his and Danielle's signals were close together around the time she disappeared. His rebuttal was that he was at work when Danielle vanished, but the phone records proved otherwise.

The messages that "Danielle" sent Stuart after bunking off from school were also analyzed. The fact that the teen only texted her uncle was troubling since she had hundreds of texts from friends and family she hadn't replied to. Plus, reading the messages, they seemed to really over-egg how brilliant Stuart was - almost like he'd written them himself.

A linguistics professor was brought in to analyze the texts and compare them to Danielle's texting style. He found several inconsistencies. In the messages to Stuart, she wrote in all caps. However, Danielle only ever wrote in lowercase. There were also spelling differences. She used the spelling "wot" instead of her usual "what." It was ascertained that Danielle didn't write these messages. Stuart Campbell did. Danielle's phone signal was close to Stuart's phone signal when the messages were sent, further cementing his guilt.

The forensic analysis of the blood-stained stockings had come back by this point. The results were sickening - both Danielle's and Stuart's DNA were mixed on the fabric.

The evidence against the man was overwhelming. So was the very real notion that Danielle was never coming back.

On August 17, 2001, Stuart was arrested for Danielle's murder. All the police had was lots and lots of circumstantial evidence. There wasn't a body. Just a stack of confirmation that Start Campbell had been harboring inappropriate, obsessive feelings toward Danielle. Her underwear, with his DNA on, was found in his home. A search of his computer found a plethora of images of young girls, some taken by him, some by other deviants. He was charged with Danielle's murder on November 14, despite the lack of a body.

Still, Stuart wouldn't give the police any information about Danielle. He refused to show them where her body was. He shut down. Perhaps he felt if there was no body, he couldn't be convicted of murder. This was a very real possibility; it's a gray area in the law that can be difficult to navigate if there's not enough evidence. Luckily for the Jones family, there was enough to find Stuart Campbell guilty of Danielle's murder.

He was given life imprisonment for murder and a 10-year sentence for abduction. He was eligible for parole at the end of 2022, and he brazenly applied for his release despite never giving the Joneses the information they so desperately need: to know where their daughter is so they can give her a burial filled with love. So they can tell her how much they love her. So they can let her know just how missed she is.

It shows a huge amount of gall on Stuart's part to assume that the parole board would grant him freedom without him offering up information about Danielle's body. Ironically, one of the courses Stuart has taken in jail is called "victim awareness." It would appear to me that his partaking in this course was futile.

All Linda and Tony want is to know where Danielle is. They wake up every day with an empty void where their daughter used to be. They have no clue how she died, how brutal it was, how long Stuart had her before he eventually murdered her. All they have to answer these macabre questions is their imagination.

The refusal of Stuart's release was bittersweet for the couple. On the one hand, a monster remains behind bars. On the other, they'd trade his sentence just to know where Danielle is and bring her home. The panel deciding if the killer could be set free set some boundaries for Stuart - he will not be suitable for release (or an open prison) until he reveals where Danielle is.

Again, if he does eventually reveal where he concealed her body, it might secure his release if the governing body no longer considers him a risk. Perhaps, one day, Stuart Campbell's desire for freedom will overrule his arrogance.

Dying To Be Popular

If you've read any of the other installments of this series, you'll know I've covered a few cases of teens committing murders. It's a truly troubling phenomenon in true crime, particularly since these types of cases are often violent, especially in comparison to some murders committed by grown adults.

The motive for these crimes is often the same, too: jealousy or mere dislike of the victim. Such a puny motive correlates with the lack of emotional intelligence these young people have. After all, when you're in your teens, you don't have the same comprehension of life as an adult, but that doesn't excuse these crimes taking place. It makes them utterly terrifying to comprehend.

Reena Virk was a rebellious 14-year-old who lived in View Royal, a historic suburb of Victoria, British Columbia. The beautiful town is home to plentiful parklands and landmarks, and mostly middle-class families inhabit the area. The Virk family set up home here, part of the blossoming Asian community that was raising their young families in the quiet town.

As Reena entered high school, Manjit and Suman Virk struggled with their teenage daughter's behavior. They were Jehovah's Witnesses, devout ones at that, so the antics their child got up to gave them plenty of sleepless nights and caused many more distressed conversations about how they could tame their rebellious daughter.

Reena felt smothered and restricted by the faith her parents wanted her to follow. She felt segregated from her peers. They had birthday parties, were given gifts on holidays, were allowed to wear whatever clothes they wanted, and were offered freedom from their parents. Reena felt like she was on the outside looking in, and her teenage peers quickly picked up on her differences.

Reena had no friends at school and was mercilessly bullied because of her dissimilarity to everyone else.

Still, Reena was desperate to be liked, to fit in, to wear cool clothes, to be invited to parties on the weekends. Nothing she did or said saw her make any connections with the people in her classes. She simply couldn't get on their wavelength. She couldn't talk to them about her favorite chart music, movies, or what make-up she wanted to buy. She didn't have anything to say on those topics because they were restricted in her household. Still, Reena figured even if she did make friends, she'd never be able to go out and socialize. Her parents simply wouldn't allow it.

She endured mistreatment every day. From having chewing gum stuck in her hair to being on the receiving end of unprovoked punches and kicks, Reena found herself to be, essentially, the school punching bag.

The only way Reena felt she could make friends was to rebel. What she did to rebel - drink alcohol, smoke, sneak out of the house - is pretty much what most teenagers do at one point or another. However, her parents couldn't cope with their young daughter's actions. They felt powerless to stop her from "acting out," and eventually, in 1996, Reena took herself to child welfare authorities with some shocking claims.

She told them her father had been sexually abusing her. When the Virk parents were confronted with this disturbing accusation, they immediately shut it down and claimed that Reena had been mixing with some unsavory teenagers who must have convinced her to say these awful things. The Virks were devastated, not only by the allegations but also because their daughter was being controlled by a group of kids who were taking advantage of her desire to be part of a group.

Still, authorities had no choice but to remove Reena from the family home to ensure her welfare. The teen girl was placed in a foster home, something her parents had figured had been the reason she'd lied about being abused. If she was in care, she was free of her parent's rules and strict lifestyle. She could come and go as she pleased, wear whatever she liked, have independence, and pocket money to spend on anything she wanted.

While it didn't quite work out this way, it certainly got Reena away from her mother and father. Eventually, Reena admitted that she'd lied about her father abusing her. For some families, this would break the relationship completely. The Virks still kept in touch with their daughter on a regular basis, however, and stayed in her life even after the extreme lengths she went to for freedom. Although the trust in their daughter had been broken, they loved Reena and wanted to be part of her life. She was being brainwashed by the new crowd she was hanging around with, her parents agreed.

Meanwhile, Reena was still in the care system and was making more friends who were also in the system. Unlike most of the other teens she was rubbing shoulders with, she wasn't in care because of her troubled behavior. She was in care because she'd made false allegations. She wasn't tough like the kids she was surrounded by. She wasn't streetwise. She didn't have the same way of thinking. She didn't understand the repercussions of getting on the wrong side of the wrong type of person. Despite seeking out these people to be her friends, there was no disguising just how sheltered Reena was in comparison.

While she was doing her best to recruit a horde of new companions, the teen girl was - knowingly or unknowingly - making lots of enemies at the same time. Socializing was something Reena was unfamiliar with, and it's clear from her actions she didn't know how to navigate her new life filled with friends.

All through school, she'd been bullied about her weight, her race, and her parent's religion. This made Reena's self-esteem hit rock bottom, so when boys began showing her attention, she felt flattered: so much so that she would sleep with them - even if they had a girlfriend. Even if that girlfriend just happened to be one of Reena's new friends.

The teen girl got a reputation for sleeping with people's boyfriends, which you can imagine made her a big target for other girls.

Eventually, the girl was given the opportunity to go back and live with her parents. She took up the offer. Although her time in foster care had gotten her away from her strict parents, she wasn't given as much freedom in care as she'd expected. Reena wrongly thought that being in a foster home would mean she could come and go at all hours, not have rules to abide by, and would be given money to buy anything she wanted. There were more home comforts at her family home, and Reena felt homesick, so being able to return was a relief. Still, she wasn't about to give up the group of friends she'd made, no matter how much her mother and father begged her to drop them.

The sneaking out and rebelliousness continued, much to the dismay of Manjit and Suman Virk.

It wasn't long before Reena decided living in the family home was unbearable again. She ended up in a youth shelter, mixing with even more streetwise kids from troubled backgrounds. She found herself back in government care but remained in contact with her parents.

Reena's lifetime of bullying had undeniably impacted her emotional well-being. Throughout school, she'd been the victim of countless attacks and verbal assaults. She'd had lies told and rumors spread about her. The downtrodden girl had noted, though, that these people were always the popular ones.

The ones who nobody dared mess with. The ones who had an assortment of friends to hang out with. Now that Reena had slowly integrated herself with these kinds of people, she figured that if she couldn't beat them, she'd join them.

One of her good friends was Missy Pleich. The two had previously met while they were young, but Missy moved away. Upon her return to View Royal, the pair met again while in the foster care system. Missy was aware of Reena's past of being bullied and victimized, but the new Reena was a far cry from the timid, shy girl she had rubbed shoulders with years earlier. She could stand up for herself verbally. She was tough - although little did Missy know, this was an act. She was merely replicating the behaviors of her peers.

As I mentioned, Reena was also known for getting herself involved with other people's boyfriends. One such boy just so happens to be Missy's love interest. As with all teen gossip, this news managed to quickly find its way back to Missy, who, as you can imagine, was none too pleased. The pair ended up having a verbal altercation, and the friendship soured rapidly.

Meanwhile, Reena was also making enemies elsewhere. Nicole Cook had been one of the girl's newfound friends until Reena took it upon herself to start spreading rumors about her.

Toward the end of 1997, she managed to obtain Nicole's phonebook and began calling the numbers in there. She randomly contacted dozens of the girl's friends and lied about her. These lies were, in hindsight, silly. She'd say Nicole had breast implants and was lying to everyone about it. Of course, if you look at these comments through teenage eyes, they would feel like an atrocity. They'd be hurtful and anger-inducing. Through adult eyes, they're witless comments that should be paid no heed.

The reason Reena did this is unknown, but I would surmise that it's a behavior she'd learned over the years. She had been a victim of rumors and lies spread and figured it was a way to assert herself as a "top dog" in order to deflect bullies away from her. It could be that, perhaps, Reena was so desperate to never be a victim again that she took on the role of bully. This is an all too common occurrence in society, sadly, whereby the victim becomes the villain, for want of a better word.

What Reena didn't consider was that the girls she was messing with were tough. Not pretend-tough like her - these young girls were hardened, had endured a life in the care system, and were streetwise. Naive Reena thought she was gaining popularity. In reality, she was making herself a target.

Nicole Cook wasn't about to let Reena get away with her disrespect. She was also friends with Missy Pleich, the other girl Reena had crossed. Together, the pair agreed that Reena needed to be taught a lesson, and that lesson would be given via their fists.

By this point, though, Reena was craving her home comforts once again. While she was technically still in the system, she was also spending nights at the family home and sleeping over.

This would give her parents some relief that their child was safe, and it would give Reena the comfort of her childhood bedroom and some time away from the teenage drama that was brewing at the care home.

On November 14, 1997, Reena had planned to spend the night with her family. However, the phone rang that afternoon, and it was Missy. She was calling to let her know there was a gathering at Craigflower Bridge that night. There'd be a ton of people there, alcohol, some weed going around, and it would be a fun night. There were often get-togethers on Friday nights, and Reena had been to a few of these pre-weekend socials. She knew they could get a bit rowdy, too, so when she was invited, she felt a pang of apprehension. Her mother felt the same, too. She begged her daughter not to go, to stay in and spend the evening as a family as planned.

However, Reena wanted to meet up with her friends. Earlier that week, the teen had heard rumors that a girl was going to get beaten up that Friday but wasn't sure who it was. A gut feeling that the girl in question might be her caused Reena to ask Missy if she was tricking her into getting a beating. "Of course not," Missy laughed, but she did admit there was a plan for someone to be beaten up that night. This put Reena at ease, and she told her mother she'd be back at 11. Suman Virk knew there was no preventing her daughter from leaving, so she accepted the arranged curfew and told Reena to be safe. "Those girls aren't your friends," she warned the teenager as she took off into the night.

This would be the last time the Virks saw their daughter alive.

The gathering was just like any other Friday night meet-up. Bottles of booze were passed around, they smoked some weed, and someone would invariably start a fire so the group would have to flee the scene.

After a few hours with the group of teens, Reena gave her parents a call to say she'd be coming home soon. It indeed had gotten rowdy, and the police had already moved them on from one place earlier that evening. There was no sign of the unnamed girl getting a beating, and Reena was tired. It was cold and damp, and nothing much was happening.

The group took shelter under the Craigflower Bridge, and the dozens of teens resumed their drinking and smoking. Reena sat down, waiting until it was time for her to head off home. Except, she wouldn't get the chance. Before she knew what was happening, she was surrounded by Missy, Nicole, and another girl called Kelly Ellard. They stood over her as she looked up at them, and the atmosphere took an ominous turn.

"Why have you been spreading rumors about me?" Nicole demanded. Five more teenagers gathered around the group, eager to see the drama unfold. "Tell me, why have you been lying?" Missy also confronted her about sleeping with her boyfriend.

Reena didn't take this opportunity to apologize or say anything that could possibly get her out of this sticky situation. In fact, she did the complete opposite. She begins calling Nicole a tirade of names, which exposes the teenager's naivety. These girls were serious and weren't afraid to use violence in any given situation. Reena was outnumbered, but that didn't stop her from talking back to Nicole. Perhaps she didn't want to be viewed as weak, as she had been for so much of her life. Regardless, as you can imagine, the backtalk didn't go down well at all.

Nicole took her lit cigarette and put it out right in the center of Reena's forehead. The searing pain left an awful mark, something that made the pack of teenagers laugh. Reena suddenly realized the danger she was in and tried to get up and leave. As she did, the whole gang began attacking her, a total of seven girls and one boy all punching and kicking her. "I'm sorry," Reena cried as the gaggle of teens pummeled her to the ground. She was utterly helpless.

Curled up in a ball, Reena sobbed, blood covering her face and hair. Kick after kick rained down on her, every part of her body being brutalized by the eight teenagers.

It was at this point a member of the group - who didn't partake in the attack - warned the gang they'd gone too far and to leave her alone. The attackers retreated and left Reena lying in the mud, blood streaming from her nose and mouth. Nicole and Missy then made their way home together, ensuring they met curfew. The rest all caught buses home, apart from Kelly Ellard, aged 15, and Warren Glowatski, who was 16.

Both of them had played an active part in beating Reena up. They left the area of the attack for a short while, during which time Reena managed to get on her feet and limp across the bridge. It was difficult for her to walk; the throbbing pain in her legs made them buckle as she attempted to make her way home. Her bus pass had been taken from her and torn up, meaning the only way the girl would get home was if she walked. It felt like an impossible task for the badly beaten girl, as she could barely make it to the north end of the bridge without collapsing.

Reena thought the worst was over. It wasn't. Kelly Ellard and Warren Glowatski were following her. Warren was no stranger to violence - he was part of a gang whereby, as part of the initiation process, he had to endure a severe beating. Much like the one he'd just inflicted on Reena. It's worth noting, though, that Warren had never met Reena until that night and had no reason to have ill feelings toward her in order to carry out such a brutal attack. Yet, here he was, following her to unleash more violence.

Kelly was unlike most of the teens who'd congregated under the bridge that night: she'd come from a stable home and hadn't endured the traumas many of her peers had. Still, she had cruel tendencies and wasn't satisfied by the beating Reena had already endured. She wanted to hurt the girl some more. So, she and Warren caught up with the limping girl as she slowly made her way across the bridge, and Kelly demanded to know if Reena was going to snitch on her. Despite Reena saying she wouldn't, this didn't appease Kelly. "She's going to snitch," she told Warren, and the pair resumed tormenting the girl.

"Take your shoes off," Kelly demanded. Reena complied, and as she did, the pair of teens lunged toward their victim once again, punching her as hard as they could in the face. The already-dried blood on Reena's face was now covered in a fresh coat of crimson.

Fifteen minutes, perhaps, doesn't sound like a long time. But this is how long the attack went on for. For a quarter of an hour, Kelly and Warren beat the girl until she was again a crying heap on the floor. They jumped up and down on her broken body, much like a child jumps on a trampoline. No area was off-limits; her head, her abdomen, and her limbs were all targeted in this vicious onslaught.

Violent Kelly then grabbed the back of Reena's head and smashed it - with as much force as she could muster - into a tree. This was the blow that rendered Reena unconscious.

The pair grabbed Reena's shoeless feet and dragged her toward the Gorge Waterway, a small tidal inlet that's deceptively deep. Before entering the water, Warren let go of the girl's ankles, thinking they'd dump the girl beside the water and take off. Kelly had a different idea.

She kept going, dragging Reena far into the waterway, only stopping when the water reached her torso. This may not sound deep, but it was enough for Reena to be completely submerged. There was no way she'd get out of there unless she miraculously regained consciousness, which, after such a barbaric and sustained attack, seemed unlikely.

By some miracle, though, Reena did wake up. She came around while Kelly attempted to drag her to her death. It seems as though the attacker had no intention of letting Reena live since, as soon as she noticed the victim coming around, she grabbed her hair, pulled her head back, and began pummeling the girl's throat. After this attack, she held Reena's head underwater until she went limp.

Warren was shoreside, watching. He didn't intervene. He didn't once tell Kelly to back off. He wasn't the one to hold the girl underwater, but he was a very willing spectator, allowing a horrific murder to take place before his eyes.

The pair took off home together, leaving Reena in the Gorge Waterway.

By this point, it was well after Reena's curfew. The Virks were understandably - and rightfully - worried, and they called the police. A full 24 hours passed. Nothing. Then another. Soon, it was 72 hours. The days blurred into one long, nauseating period of torture for the Virks.

The distraught parents even visited the care home where Missy and Nicole were and asked them if they'd been with their daughter or had any information about Reena's whereabouts. They had nothing to tell them, the teens said. They had no clue where Reena was or who she might be with.

After this, the girls decide there may be some evidence of the attack still lying around Craigflower Bridge. They took themselves to the crime scene and picked up some of Reena's torn clothing that was strewn among empty bottles and cigarette butts. They handed the items to another girl at the care home, who was uninvolved with Reena's attack. She was told to hide the items. She did as she was told.

The gang of violent teens had agreed with one another that they'd keep their vile act between them. Nobody but those there that night could ever know what happened to Reena Virk. They made a pact and resumed their lives. Some of them attended Shoreline Middle School, and this is where rumors started swirling.

It seems one of the gang - although nobody can be sure who - began telling outsiders the gory secret. Maybe to brag, maybe to assert themselves as someone to fear, or maybe they just couldn't help but share the gossip; whatever the reason, someone broke the pact pretty quickly.

By now, it was day eight of Reena's vanishing, and the police were at a loss. Nobody was coming forward with any information. Still, the rumors had gotten back to law enforcement, but they couldn't make arrests based on rumors. Teenagers are renowned for making up stories and urban legends, so there was nothing the police could do without either solid evidence or a body.

On the eighth day, an awful discovery confirmed the Virk's worst nightmare had come true. Reena's partially clothed body was found floating in the waterway. The heartbroken parents knew their gut feeling about Reena's new companions was right, and waves of guilt and anger flooded their muddled thoughts.

Could they have stopped her from going out that night? What could they have done to spare their child from enduring such an awful death?

Two days later, her autopsy was carried out. It revealed a lot of disturbing details, something the Virk family had to endure being listed out. The findings included Reena had a sneaker print on the back of her brain - that's how much force she had been beaten with. Her entire body had been brutalized, resembling that of a high-speed car crash victim. It was concluded that it was highly unlikely that Reena would have ever survived the attack had she not been held underwater and drowned.

The rumors police had been hearing turned out, for once, to be true.

Despite the initial pact not to "rat" on each other, that promise was quickly broken by the teens without much interrogation at all. Six of the seven girls who partook in the initial attack on Reena were Missy Pleich, Kelly Ellard, Nicole Cook, Nicole Patterson, Courtney Keith, and Gail Ooms. Another girl, who wasn't named, was found unfit for trial. Warren Glowatski was the only male detained.

All of the members except Warren and Kelly were charged with assault causing bodily harm. They were tried in youth court and found guilty.

Warren and Kelly were tried in an adult court, despite being underage, due to the extreme violence used in their fatal beating of Reena.

In June 1999, Warren was convicted of second-degree murder and given life in prison. Parole was a possibility after seven years. The following March, Kelly Ellard was convicted of second-degree murder and handed to life in prison with parole a possibility after five years.

While in prison, it seems Warren showed genuine remorse for his part in Reena's murder. He took part in programs geared toward restoring justice and took a keen interest in a program that aimed to connect offenders with their victims. The Virks met with Warren during his time in prison, and the young killer expressed his sorrow and regret at what happened in 1997.

He admitted to them that he had no reason to kill Reena, no genuine motive, just a wayward aggression that resulted in an innocent teenager's violent death. Surprisingly, the parents hugged their daughter's murderer before leaving, something I think few of us would be strong enough to do. They say you forgive someone not for *them* but for yourself. To let go of all the hurt, pain, and anger toward the person that hurt you is freeing. I can but assume this is why the Virks were able to accept Warren's apology and grant him their forgiveness.

Warren's 2010 parole bid was even supported by Reena's parents, which is perhaps why it was successful. Warren has remained out of trouble with the law since his release.

In contrast, it seems Kelly Ellard had a different time in prison. She didn't accept her guilt or the major part she played in Reena's murder; she flouted prison rules by taking drugs and got pregnant behind bars during a conjugal visit. She was given a chance at day parole in 2020 to see if she could be reintegrated into society. This was suspended after Kelly failed to report episodes of domestic violence.

Little has been reported about the remainder of the gang since their sentencing and subsequent releases. I'd like to presume this is because they've managed to live full lives, and they're upstanding members of society who don't have run-ins with the law. Still, the knowledge of what they did back in 1997 surely must haunt them: the fact they stripped a naive teenager away from her doting parents in such a cruel way. The way in which, for over a week, they simply got on with their lives, knowing they took someone else's for no real reason.

Reena Virk died to fit in, quite literally. The youths sniffed out her differences and her weaknesses and surrounded her that fateful night like hungry wolves. She found herself in a place she ought never to have been in, just to make friends and be popular, making this tale all the more heartbreaking. It gives a tragic meaning to the phrase "dying to be popular."

Bound By Heartlessness

Serial killer couples are rare, making cases like this utterly frightening. When you consider the monstrous violence and cruelty inflicted on Gerald and Charlene Gallego's young victims, you add another layer of depravity to these crimes.

You may have heard of other killer couples like Karla Homolka and Paul Bernardo or Myra Hindley and Ian Brady. In those cases, the women, despite being active participants in the murders they were found guilty of, wound up blaming their partners for instigating the crimes. The females would say they participated in the sickening crimes to appease their lover and claim they were also a victim of their partner's reign of abuse.

Perhaps they are somewhat telling the truth. It was proven that Paul Bernardo would beat his wife Karla mercilessly. She'd often be seen with black eyes and a swollen face. She was known to do anything at all to please him. So much so that she offered her younger sister to him as one of their victims. It's hard to find much empathy for the woman when you learn about all the atrocious things she did to young girls to maintain her twisted husband's happiness. In my view, she certainly began as Bernardo's victim, but when she became an eager contributor to the abuse of the young women he'd bring home, that label was torn off her. She never sought help, never went to the police, and helped him cover up the crimes they committed.

The case I'm going to cover has similarities to the Homolka and Bernardo crimes.

Gerald Gallego was born in sunny Sacramento, California on July 17, 1946. His family on both sides were familiar with run-ins with the law. Gerald would continue this decades-long familial tradition, starting at a young age. He exhibited disturbing signs of degeneracy from a young age, but considering this was the norm in his lineage, nothing was done to rectify it. His father was out of the picture by the time Gerald turned nine after being executed in the gas chamber for a string of crimes, including the murder of a police officer.

Still, Gerald's life had a steady stream of male influence - but that's not a good thing. To make ends meet, his mother began sex work, which brought an influx of men into the family home. Barely any of these men gave the young boy the time of day, and the ones that did would beat the boy bloody. Some of them even took advantage of the child to satisfy their perverse desires. If it wasn't clients abusing young Gerald, it was his mother's latest boyfriend. His mother - the woman who ought to have protected her boy - would often abuse Gerald, too.

There were no hugs, no words of comfort, no real time spent with the boy. He was left to fend for himself and learn about the world independently. Sadly, the only world he was exposed to was one of neglect and abuse. It's no surprise, then, that Gerald would go on to continue this cycle.

His first run-in with the law came at the age of 10. He robbed a neighbor's home, possibly for food. The child was frequently left unfed, although his reasons for the crime were not investigated. By the age of 12, he was caught for his first sexual crime, although it's unlikely this was the first time he engaged in such an offense. He was arrested for sexually assaulting a six-year-old. Despite Gerald's young age, his mind was already working at a deviant level. He spent some time at a youth facility for this felony and was back on the streets by the time he was a teenager.

As you can imagine, the issues Gerald had weren't rectified. If anything, his time in the boys-only facility merely exposed him to new, depraved ideas that he would go on to carry out upon his release.

Run-ins with the law became a constant in Gerald's young life, mostly for theft. He participated in an armed robbery, which saw him spend some time in a juvenile offenders school, which he was released from in 1963. The criminal was now 16 years old, and shortly after his release, he met a 21-year-old woman to whom he quickly proposed. The pair married in December of that year. The following spring, their daughter was born.

With Gerald being violent and abusive, the marriage was doomed from the start. Not long after baby Krista entered the world, the pair split up. Somehow, despite his criminal background and deeply unhinged behavior, Gerald managed to obtain custody of his young daughter. This decision by the courts would expose the child to her father's abuse, both verbal and sexual. Her only respite came when her father sent her to live with her mother, although she would still frequently be sent to visit her dad - her abuser.

Four years later, in 1966, Gerald married again. The marriage lasted just short of a month. His fondness for beating the women in his life meant his new bride fled the relationship almost as quickly as she entered it. I can only applaud the young woman for doing so since so many women, especially in the 60s, would stick around and try to make the marriage work. Fortunately, the woman knew there was no "trying to make it work" with a man who would threaten her with knives and beat her relentlessly.

Gerald's life of crime continued amidst a string of failed love affairs until, in 1969, he once again found himself in jail for armed robbery. He was handed five years in prison for his role in the crime. No matter how much time Gerald was jailed or how many reformation classes he took, nothing could veer him off the tracks of corruption he was on.

After his release, he got married a third time, but again, the partnership was short-lived. Again, his penchant for extreme violence saw his third bride run and never look back from the marriage. Gerald didn't seem to want to control his temper and lust for power over women. This might explain his need to marry his girlfriends quickly after meeting - to secure their place in his life as his subordinate. To make it harder for them to leave. It's no surprise, then, that he got hitched again to wife number four in 1969.

This marriage took place in Reno, the biggest little city in the world, a miniature Las Vegas. The whirlwind romance, of course, soured quickly, but not before Gerald fathered a child with his 19-year-old bride. In a clever move, she took off with her unborn baby and never let the father near her. Had she not taken this precaution, there's little doubt the child would have met the same fate as his first daughter, Krista, who endured years of sexual abuse.

It took Gerald five more years before he'd marry again - a record amount of time for the serial groom to snare a new bride. This marriage lasted just over two years, by which time Gerald met the woman who would go on to be his partner in crime, quite literally.

Charlene Williams was a twice-divorced young woman from a good family with a stable upbringing, the opposite of Gerald's childhood. Charlene was noticeably intelligent, had achieved high grades at school, and was articulate when she spoke. However, as she entered her teenage years, she hit a rebellious phase.

As she became a young woman, her parents despaired as their daughter's behavior changed due to her alcohol and drug use. Charlene appeared to be on a downward spiral before she met Gerald, who possibly sensed her weakness and naivety.

Charlene was, what you'd call at the time, promiscuous. She got herself labeled as such, although in much crasser terms. Wherever she went, be it to work or social events, other females despised her. They wouldn't dare leave her alone in the company of their husbands for fear the young woman would seduce them. This happened on a number of occasions, and engaging in an affair with a married man wasn't off-limits for Charlene.

Despite her many dalliances with men, Charlene also took an especially intense interest in other women. She would often ask her partners if they could add a woman to their courtship and was known to ask the married men she dated if they could ask their wives to join them in bed. This led to her being rejected by these men, who were scared off by Charlene's interest in their spouses.

Perhaps the young woman felt misunderstood. Perhaps she was looking for comfort in all the wrong places. After two failed marriages and more flings that ended in heartbreak, Charlene decided to end her life. The pain of rejection and perhaps being confused by her feelings fueled her desire to no longer be here. Still, the attempt at her life was unsuccessful. Shortly thereafter, the 21-year-old met Gerald Gallego at a casino in Sacramento. It was love at first sight.

The women before Charlene had all fled pretty early on in Gerald's relationships. Not Charlene - whatever problems she faced with Gerald, and there were plenty of them - would be something she'd try to fix. She endured his abuse, both physical and verbal, without so much as a threat of leaving. She did whatever he asked in a bid to please her lover, even engaging in painful sexual acts. Gerald enjoyed hurting his lover, both in and out of bed, and would act out his violent fantasies on Charlene.

Soon, inflicting pain on Charlene became boring for the vicious man. To reignite his excitement, Gerald met a young exotic dancer one evening and convinced her to go home with him. He persuaded the woman to sleep with him and Charlene but with one big caveat: they were, under no circumstances, allowed to touch one another. The women had to focus solely on Gerald. They abided by his rules that night, but the women, unbeknown to the man who introduced them, would take a liking to one another.

Of course, they couldn't express their feelings in front of Gerald. They'd have to meet up behind his back, which they did.

Gerald came home one evening to find his lover in bed with the dancer he had brought home. As you can imagine, this caused the man to fly into a red-hot rage. He flung the young dancer out of the window with force before turning his attention to Charlene. She endured a brutal beating for her indiscretion.

After this incident, Gerald would abstain from sleeping with Charlene. He told her it was because he'd lost all desire to do so after catching her in bed with someone else. It had made him impotent.

However, Charlene didn't believe this was the case; she suspected his lack of interest in her was because he was sleeping with other women. Gerald's job as a bartender meant he met dozens of women every night, and since he often didn't get home until late, she guessed he was out with these other females. It would explain his lack of interest in her, at least.

Somehow, though, Charlene managed to fall pregnant with Gerald's child. It's unknown if Charlene knew Gerald abused his daughter, but it's hard to believe it would be something he'd try hard to keep from her. If she did know, she must've realized that her child would likely meet the same fate as Krista. When Gerald found out he was going to be a father again, though, he demanded his partner get rid of the baby. Charlene complied.

In Autumn 1978, Gerald had a new proposition for his browbeaten partner. Things were getting boring, he said; he wasn't satisfied. He didn't want to leave her, but if things didn't improve, he'd have no choice but to. The only thing Charlene could do to retain her relationship was to eagerly agree to Gerald's request to kidnap a pair of "sex slaves." There was no denying for Charlene that the idea gave her a genuine spark of excitement - she had confusing feelings towards other women, and this would be a good chance to explore those emotions in the confines of her relationship.

The pair agreed it was a great idea. They hopped in their car and drove the Sacramento streets in search of the perfect pair to swipe in broad daylight. It wasn't too long before the twisted couple found two young girls they liked the look of. Charlene would be the one to approach the girls, it was agreed since females were less inclined to be scared off by other women.

Charlene pulled up beside 17-year-old Rhonda Scheffler and 16-year-old Kippi Vaught. "Hey," the woman smiled at the teens, "Do you want to join us for a smoke in the van?" she asked the girls. This wasn't an offer the two teenagers got every day. Plus, they felt they could trust Charlene since she was older and had a warm smile when she spoke.

The opportunity to get high for free in the safety of a van? They were in. It would be a decision that led them to their horrific deaths. When Charlene agreed to carry out this awful crime, perhaps she didn't know just how brutal it was going to be. Whether or not she regretted saying yes to the kidnappings didn't matter - she partook in it anyway.

Once the two girls were lured into the back of the van, they discovered a pistol-wielding man was in there. They had no chance to run - his gun was being pointed at them alternately. They'd be shot in the head before they got more than five feet away from the van. Gerald ordered the girls into the back of the vehicle, where he tied the teens up with strong tape, binding their hands and feet together. They were rendered immobile.

Charlene sat in the back while Gerald hopped in the driver's seat, looking for a desolate area to carry out his depraved compulsions. He found somewhere suitable in Baxter, California, and parked up, turned off the engine, and opened the van doors. Charlene sat upright as the two victims cried to be set free, their wrists and ankles red raw from the tight tape that bound them.

The assaults carried out on Rhonda and Kippi lasted through the night. He violated the girls until the following morning.

When he was done, Gerald drove to a quiet area just outside of downtown Sacramento. He ordered the tied-up teens out of his van and marched them into a nearby field. Any hopes of being set free may have crossed the girls' minds, but considering they'd just endured hours of violence at this sadistic man's hands, perhaps any hope had been beaten out of them.

While ordering them through the field, Gerald attacked both girls with a tire iron without warning. He beat both of them to the floor, bashing them over the head with blind rage before taking out his pistol. Each girl got a bullet in the head.

Gerald placed his gun in his back pocket, picked up the bloodied tire iron, and began walking back to his van, where Charlene sat watching.

Unbeknown to Gerald, though, the bullet he'd used on Kippi hadn't penetrated her skull. In fact, it had only grazed it. She was battered and beaten for sure, but when she saw her attacker leaving, she made a break for it. She didn't bank on the murderous man to look back at his victims, which he did just as Kippi jumped to her feet, readying herself to run to safety. For daring to live, Kippi got three more bullets in her skull.

Gerald then jumped in the van next to Charlene, who was clearly excited about the events that had just taken place. "Drive," the killer ordered his submissive accomplice. She started the engine, and they fled the scene, euphoric with the acts they'd just committed. The feelings she felt while carrying out crimes with the man she loved were indescribable; there was no doubt she enjoyed doing it. Any trepidation Charlene may have had vanished. She was a willing accomplice.

The pair were keen to relive the rush of the first crime. Often, criminals will wait a while before committing their next murder in order to avoid finding themselves in trouble with the law. They wait for the outrage of their first crime to die down before embarking on a new victim. Gerald and Charlene laid low for a while, although they agreed they'd soon capture a new pair of girls.

In the meantime, the bodies of Rhonda and Kippi were discovered by two men, who no doubt will ever get the disturbing discovery wiped from their memory. The decomposing bodies, bloodied and mangled, were soon identified as the two teen girls.

This didn't faze the killer couple. They got married quickly after their first crime together. It seems their evil acts bound them even tighter together.

Shortly after that, Krista filed sexual abuse charges against Gerald. The charges were highly disturbing. Of course, Gerald likely knew there was an abundance of evidence to prove his abuse of Krista, notably due to his violent ways. Her body had been ravaged by the brute she'd been forced to spend time with - the one who ought to have taken care of her and protected her. In a bid to flee the lengthy rap sheet against him, Gerald told Charlene to pack up - they were heading to Texas.

The man also assumed a new identity around this time, in December 1978. He called himself Stephen Feil.

With a brand new identity, Gerald decided he wanted to "get some more girls." Charlene obliged, as she always did. The pair chose not to scour their new home area in Texas and headed to Reno, Nevada, to look for some more victims. Perhaps they didn't want to attract attention to themselves in Texas, or perhaps they knew Nevada's roads and secluded areas; whatever the reason, they chose Washoe County Fair to seek out the newest abductees.

Gerald sent Charlene to mingle in the bustling crowd and scope out girls who would match his type. She took off, smiling at the pretty teen girls and gauging their response.

After walking around the fair for a while, she spotted Brenda Judd, 14, and Sandra Colley, 13. She strolled up to the girls, who were simply there to have a good time and meet some new friends, and asked them if they wanted a job for some quick cash. Charlene had a bulk of paper advertisements she needed to hand out and stick on the windshields of the fairgoers' parked cars.

It was easy money, by the sounds of it, so the two girls jumped at the chance. They'd need to go to Charelne's van to collect the stack of adverts. The teens followed the older woman, excited at the prospect of earning their own money for once.

Charlene opened the van doors and crouched inside. Gerald was there yet again with the pistol in hand. "Get in," Charlene demanded. It was clear that Charlene was keen to be a much more active participant in the sick crimes she'd planned with her husband this time. The terrified teens got in the back of the van, where Gerald taped their hands and feet at gunpoint. Charlene jumped in the driver's seat and sped off, looking for a good, quiet spot to park.

Meanwhile, Gerald sexually assaulted both girls in the back of the van. Charlene would frequently take her eyes off the road and watch in the rearview mirror. Where most of us would be filled with disgust and anger at what was going on back there, the perverted woman took great joy in what she was seeing.

Eventually, Charlene parked up on the dry lake bed Humboldt Sink. The abuse of the girls would continue with the woman's involvement, where she'd force the victims to carry out acts on one another. Gerald wasn't there at this point - he was in the front catching up on sleep. Still, Charlene spent hours abusing and tormenting the girls before Gerald awoke and demanded their demise.

Sandra was first. She was dragged from the van and repeatedly hit over her head with a shovel. Charlene watched as Sandra fell to the floor, her face smacking the dusty ground. Once satisfied the girl was dead, they repeated the sickening act on Brenda. Gerald dug a large grave, threw the naked bodies in, and covered it up. He rolled a large rock over the makeshift tomb to ensure it wasn't found, and there was no chance either girl was getting out.

Although the teens had been reported missing, they were labeled as runaways. No search for them took place, nobody was looking for them, and their bodies were left to decompose in the blistering heat of the lake bed.

The couple couldn't manage long in Texas. After just a year, they returned to their old stomping ground of Sacramento. Gerald didn't revert back to his true identity. He didn't want to face up to the allegations brought against him by his daughter, after all. The Gallegos became the Feils. Gerald got a job at a bar, which brought in a little money but had Charlene on edge. She knew what her husband was like, and pretty soon, he was staying out later and later, way past the bar's closing time. Sure enough, he was having an affair with a young woman called Patti.

However, having a surplus of women didn't quell Gerald's desire to take young victims against their will. In the spring of 1980, he woke Charlene up one morning and demanded she get up and get dressed. They were going out. "I want a girl," he demanded. Charlene got up and pulled a vest and some jeans on before joining her husband in his van.

The search was always the same: driving around until they found girls whom Gerald liked the look of. Sometimes, it would take hours. They passed a bookstore on their travels and, just as they did, noticed Karen Twiggs and Stacy Redican vacating the premises. The 17-year-olds were exactly what Gerald wanted. "Park up," he demanded of his eagerly obedient wife. "Go get them." As ordered, Charlene got the girls under the guise of smoking some weed in the back of her van. Once the teens got to the van, again Gerald was crouched in the back with his trusty pistol.

As before, Charlene took the driver's seat while her husband carried out his sick acts of depravity in the back. When she pulled up eventually, Charlene was even more involved in the victims' abuse this time. Hours passed, and as soon as Gerald decided, the teen's time was up. They were expendable to him. He'd kill them and just go out and get more when he felt the urge. He was such a cold, heartless individual whose frustratingly subservient wife enabled his twisted urges.

Karen and Stacy were taken to a desolate woodland in Nevada and buried. Gerald didn't do a thorough job of this since when the girls were found in late 1980, coyotes had dug them up and ravaged their corpses. Still, it was ascertained their death was caused by blunt force trauma. Forensics wasn't anywhere near as good in the 80s as it is today - not even marginally. Still, it was discovered the girls had been raped prior to their untimely end.

The following month, Charlene had some news for her husband - she was pregnant. It's unknown if Charlene welcomed this news, although there's no discrepancy as to how Gerald felt. This time, he wouldn't demand an abortion.

To maintain their fake identities, the killer couple got married again that summer. This time, they were Mr. and Mrs. Stephen Feil. Mere days later, Gerald told his wife he wanted a new pair of victims.

The Feils set out on June 7, 1980, and found Linda Aguilar walking along the road in Port Orford, Oregon. She stuck her thumb out when she saw the couple's van heading toward her and would make a grave error of judgment by accepting Gerald's offer of a lift. Initially, the couple sat and spoke with Linda as they drove, but Gerald soon couldn't help but pull out his trademark pistol. It seems he was unable to carry out an abduction without it, despite having a second pair of hands to help him.

Linda Aguilar met the same fate as the young women before her. The 21-year-old was four months pregnant at the time of her murder. After raping the victim, Gerald dragged Linda from the van, picked up a rock, and pummeled her until he felt there was no chance she'd survive. Even so, he decided to strangle the woman afterward just to be sure - he didn't want to leave any witnesses alive. Then, the pair buried her close to Gold Beach, Oregon, before fleeing the scene.

What they didn't know was that Linda didn't die. Despite Gerald breaking her skull before burying her underneath a heavy pile of sand, Linda was still alive. She awoke in her sandy grave, understandably terrified and confused. In her bid to make her way out of her burial site, she panicked and began ingesting the sand that covered her. She almost made it out alive - almost. Tragically, she died while trying to get free; she suffocated to death. She was found two weeks later by tourists on the beach.

The crimes were becoming more and more frequent. Gerald wanted to kidnap some girls every month by this point, and that's just what he and his wife did to celebrate his 34th birthday. This time, they were more brazen in their choice of victim. The pair knew the woman they abducted since she was a barmaid at a drinking hole they frequented. They'd been served beers by the woman they bundled into their van. It shows the extra callousness of the couple. Not only could they abduct and carry out horrific acts on victims they didn't know, but they could just as easily do it toward someone they were familiar with.

Virginia Mochel was leaving work on a humid night on July 17, 1980. Before she knew it, Gerald had her bound in the back of his van. Charlene was at the wheel as always, glancing in the back at what her dear husband was doing to the woman who'd just served them a pitcher hours earlier. Yet again, the victim endured hours of torment at the hands of her captors before being discarded. Prior to her death, the ordeal she endured was so traumatic she begged the couple to just kill her.

Gerald tied some fishing line around her neck and, once he was sure she was no longer breathing, dumped his victim's lifeless body at a pond in Yolo County. It took months for Virginia's body to be found, and although she'd decomposed rapidly, the fishing line remained around her neck.

The couple was sated until November 1980. Then, as he always did, Gerald began getting "that feeling again." Charlene never said no to her husband. This time, however, it would be different from their other murders. The pair took off on a hunt, passing 22-year-old Craig Miller and his 21-year-old fiancée Mary Sowers wandering the streets in the early morning hours. The young couple had been out partying and were a little worse for wear.

Unusually, this time, the Gallegos chose a couple that weren't two females. Perhaps there were slim pickings that night, or Gerald wanted to know how it felt to kill a man. Regardless, like all their kidnappings before, they forced the couple into their vehicle and took off. The manner in which they got their victims in the van was certainly bolder than their previous crimes, though. Gerald exited the vehicle himself on this occasion instead of taking himself to the back of his van and waiting with his pistol. He walked right up to the tipsy couple, stuck his gun in their face, and told them to get in the back.

Such a shameless and brash act, carried out in plain view, was witnessed by the couple's friends who were walking nearby. Of course, they noted down the license plate number, unbeknown to the Gallegos. Things would take a tragic turn before the witnesses went to the police with the events they'd seen.

The victims were taken to a desolate area where Craig was told to get out of the vehicle. As he did, Gerald raised his pistol, shooting the young man three times in the back of his head. Mary was forced to watch.

Satisfied the man was dead, the killers did something they'd never done before: they drove their remaining victim back to their apartment. It seems the duo had suddenly gotten very flagrant in their crimes, almost as if they believed they were untouchable. They didn't know it yet, but they certainly weren't untouchable. Still, they had Mary in their bedroom, and the young woman had to endure hours of assaults at the hands of her sick captors. When they were done, the couple drove her to a quiet area, and just like her fiancée, Mary was killed with three bullets to the head.

By this time, the police were onto them. Authorities didn't know the true extent of what the Gallegos had been doing, but their license plate number had been handed to them with a troubling tale of kidnap. It wasn't long before the couple were cuffed while they were at a bank waiting for Charlene's mother to send them some money. The police also managed to obtain a warrant to search the Gallegos property, including their van.

They found some questionable items but nothing entirely conclusive. Still, Charlene confessed to the police without much interrogation at all. It showed a stark difference to the subservient woman who'd do anything her wicked husband told her to do.

Did she want out? Had she gotten sick of always having to be ready to pick up another girl? Had her conscience finally found her? Or, perhaps, did she think the jig was up, and Charlene wanted to gain the upper hand - and a plea bargain - by confessing all?

We'll never know, but Charlene confessed to all their crimes - even admitting to the murders of Brenda Judd and Sandra Colley, who were assumed to have run away.

Two months after their arrests, Charlene gave birth to a baby boy, also named Gerald. He was handed over to Charlene's mother and father to take care of since it was apparent the woman wouldn't be walking free for a very long time. Neither would Gerald Sr. The Californian public was so sickened by the crimes they raised almost $30,000 to help aid his prosecution. With Charlene's evidence, there was little Gerald could offer as a rebuttal. She knew where the bodies had been buried, how they'd been killed, and confessed in such great detail there was no doubt the pair had committed these sick acts.

In June 1983, Gerald was sentenced to death. Later that year, Charlene was given sixteen years and eight months behind bars. A super lenient sentence, you're perhaps thinking, one that was obtained by going against her former partner in crime. However, if the plea bargain wasn't offered, it could be that the killer couple were set free to kill again and again. Charlene may never have given the evidence needed to secure a trial if the plea bargain hadn't been put on the table.

Gerald tried to appeal his sentence as much as was allowed. It was always denied. While awaiting his execution, he died of cancer in 2002, aged 56. Throughout his teens and adult life, Gerald was a violent, sexually deranged man who preyed on women to gratify his sick and twisted desires. No doubt, if he hadn't been caged, this repetitive behavior would have continued with or without Charlene.

Charlene was released from prison in July 1997. She changed her identity and resides in Sacramento to this day. Still, despite her ability to habitate where she and her former husband raped and murdered many young girls and a young man, she asserts her regret and sorrow. She says she, too, was a victim of Gerald. Some victims died, she says, and she's the one who got away.

She insists she never killed anybody and that her partaking in the crimes was just to pacify her violent husband. He would beat and rape her, too, she says, and there was no help for her. Charlene says she's proud that she managed to put her ex on death row.

You may brush these statements off as empty words, although I feel there is some truth to them. I do believe she was abused by Gerald, too, but I don't believe the only way she could have escaped with her life is by watching him take many others. I do believe she didn't physically kill anybody, but I don't believe she's absolved of the horrid deaths of the young people who died at the killer couple's hands.

By all accounts, Charlene now devotes much of her time to charity work and desires to live a life under the radar. She still fears the Gallego family and doesn't want them to know her new identity.

Murderous Matriarch

Some women are just born to be a mother. It's not an easy task, nor does it come naturally to everyone. Parenthood is tough. Nobody ever gets it "right," but some mothers and fathers can navigate it better than others. Still, even for those who got it wrong all too frequently, it wasn't out of malice or a lack of love.

Louise Porton is the opposite of someone who should have ever even considered motherhood. Just about everything else came before her young babies, who she felt got in the way of her life. The way she rectified this apparent conundrum wasn't to seek help or to go to authorities and admit she couldn't care for her children. It was by ending their heartbreakingly short lives.

There's not a great deal of information out there about this case despite how horrific and shocking it is. Still, the essence of this series is to cover such crimes, not letting them slip into obscurity as time goes by, and this is a case that should certainly be remembered.

Louise Porton was born in 1997 in Warwickshire, the West Midlands of England. She was part of a close-knit family who spent a lot of time together. Cousins, aunts, and grandparents were a mainstay in Louise's young life, and she was often made to visit them with her mother. For most children, this is something to look forward to, a chance to see extended family and perhaps play with the younger family members who are also there. Not Louise - it seems she resented having a big family who took an interest in each other's lives.

Her cousins would be wary of her whenever she was made to join her mother in visiting their home. As a youngster, it seems Louise, for whatever reason, was an angry, troubled child. She would lash out at her young cousins for no apparent explanation. One of her cousins would describe how Louise would hurt them but make sure nobody was looking when she did it. This is a disturbing piece of information since it shows just how conniving she was, even from a young age.

It also exposes that Louise knew what she was doing was wrong. It's not like she was a child with uncontrollable anger - she controlled it and only carried it out when she was sure she wouldn't be caught. She would carry these sneaky traits with her into adulthood.

Even as she entered her teens, she didn't warm to any of her family, be it those around the same age as her, those younger or older; she seemed to despise all of them. She would threaten to smash her cousin's face in, all the while smiling at her mother and acting as if everything was okay. She unnerved those closest in age to her.

The family did come in useful for some things for Louise, though. She began taking money from her grandmother as a teen. She exploited her mother for money, too, and would get upset if she couldn't obtain the cash she so desperately wanted.

She'd unleash her nasty side if she got caught, and despite this, her family would often let these things slide. It was clear that Louise was harboring some challenging traits, but these were swept under the rug. Either that or the red flags were simply not seen.

As with most teen girls, Louise became interested in pursuing relationships. However, her feelings towards boys weren't innocent crushes or desiring to be taken on dates; she was willing to sleep with any boy who showed her some interest. Her mental relationship with the opposite sex wasn't a healthy one. She sought out validation from all the wrong people in all the wrong ways and found herself flitting from boy to boy, being treated with little value as she did. Eventually, she figured she could combine her two biggest interests - money and boys. This began Louise's journey into sex work.

Around this time, Louise's grandmother fell ill. Despite the family begging Louise to go visit her grandmother - it could be her last opportunity to do so, they warned her - she point-blank refused. Of course, this meant the older woman sadly died without seeing her beloved granddaughter one last time, but it's hard to believe that this fazed Louise since she didn't bother going to the funeral, either.

This caused Louise's family to shun her somewhat. They felt like the teenager decided her grandmother was of no use to her anymore, so she didn't need to keep up the guise of caring about her.

By the time she was 18, Louise had found out she was pregnant. She obtained a council house in preparation for the birth of her first child, Lexi Draper. Shortly after, the teen found out she was pregnant again, and she gave birth to her second little girl, Scarlett Vaughan.

Between 2016 and 2017, Louise lived near Walsall, in the West Midlands. During this period, she would go out, party, socialize, and meet men despite having two very young babies to look after. Her landlady would often be left with the two children while Louise was out, and although this angered the owner of the building, she felt she had no choice. Louise would be going out and doing her own thing regardless. The landlady would later say that Louise would do everything she could to avoid having her kids with her.

Not only that, but the landlady noticed Louise was very short and snappy with her children. She'd swear at them and become visibly agitated by them. It was clear to see she resented motherhood.

The children's father wasn't really in the picture. He had only met the eldest, Lexi, and before he got the opportunity to meet Scarlett, Louise moved back to Warwickshire. In fact, she refused to give Scarlett his last name - she gave the young child another man's surname with whom she'd been in an on-off relationship. The biological father said the move was calculated to make sure he'd not be able to see his children.

Meanwhile, Louise was doubling down on making money through sex work. Despite claiming government benefits, she couldn't quell her desire for bundles of cash.

There's no denying we all like money - it brings comfort, stability, and luxuries here and there. But it shouldn't be all-consuming when it comes at the expense of spending time with your two extremely young children. For Louise, it was. She'd spend hours on her phone, dating apps, chat websites, and selling her services to those who might be interested.

Some just wanted pictures or videos for cash. Others required her to leave her children and take off out of the house to make money. Either way, she was neglecting her youngsters. She would even offer clients to visit her home. Bear in mind she was living in a one-bedroom flat - there would be very little space between her clients and her kids. Her want for money - not *need* for money - came before her children.

The men she'd invite over were complete strangers. She had no way of vetting them before they came to her home. She often told prospective customers that she had two small children at her property, so they'd have to be quiet. These men could have had fiendish desires and have been encouraged by the fact Louise was living alone with her two babies. The mother had incredibly poor decision-making skills at best. At worst, she was willfully neglecting her children and putting them in harm's way.

The worst was yet to come, however. The basic components of motherhood - the desire to protect, nurture, and comfort - were lost upon Louise.

On January 2, 2018, Lexi was rushed to hospital due to having difficulty breathing. She was stabilized and sent back home with Louise but was rushed back in just two days later, suffering the same symptoms. The doctors who saw little Lexi reduced the breathing problems to a chest infection.

It was noted that Louise seemed unbothered about her baby's well-being while paramedics tended to the sick child. She was clearly a young mother, so it was put down to emotional immaturity: perhaps she was unable or unwilling to confront the scary possibility that her daughter was sick with an unknown illness. The reality was much more sinister, though.

All the while doctors were taking a look at Lexi, Louise was texting prospective clients, working out prices for her services, and discussing what pictures she was going to send them. She even took herself off to the hospital lavatory and took nude snaps of herself in exchange for a few pounds. There is no excuse for this - she simply didn't care that her daughter was suffering.

After all, she was the one who'd inflicted the breathing problems on her child.

Before leaving the hospital, Louise slipped her number to the security guard, and the pair exchanged a number of flirty exchanges. It seems Louise wasn't averse to picking up prospective clients, no matter how dire the situation.

A few days later. Louise made a call to 999. She was quiet on the call, and when the handler asked if the toddler was breathing, Louise bluntly replied, "No." When the handler asked Louise who the baby was, Louise replied, "Lexi, she's three." I found it odd that she didn't reply, "She's my daughter, Lexi." She distanced herself from the child immediately, was matter-of-fact in her tone, and had very little concern in her voice.

The ambulance arrived swiftly after the call was made, but paramedics made a shocking discovery. Little Lexi was dead and had been for some time. Hours before the call for help had been made. Louise was informed of her daughter's passing and, again, showed no real concern. Sure, she was sniffly and quiet, but she didn't shed a tear. We all deal with trauma in different ways. Some of us need time to process the traumatic thing we're going through. Some of us crumble into a heap as the enormity of the situation hits us. Something didn't sit right about Louise's reaction - or lack thereof.

Louise was taken to the hospital with her child, yet again, she was messaging men on various dating apps and chat apps. She accepted dozens and dozens of friend requests from men in the hours after her child had died.

During their conversations, she would even tell some of these men that her daughter had passed away. When they expressed their condolences, Louise insisted, "It's alright."

For most mothers, losing a child would be a pivotal moment. One you'd never understand, an event you'd forever question the unfairness of. The grief would be overwhelming, and again, I understand people deal with grief in different ways. But if Louise Porton had truly cared about her child, how could she possess the ability to have banter with random men and discuss meeting up with them?

Again, the reason for this lack of care was that Louise was the reason her child was dead. She had purposefully ended her firstborn's life. She didn't even care enough to make it seem like she cared about her death.

This was noted a few weeks after Lexi's passing, too. The funeral arranger spotted Louise laughing and joking on a video call with an unknown man. There's no law against this, but it's strange behavior from a recently bereaved mother.

Life was business as usual for Louise after this. She didn't seem to care at all about the death of her child. Just two weeks later, it seemed tragedy would strike again.

Louise made a call to 111 - the non-emergency number in the U.K. - to seek advice on her daughter Scarlett, who was unwell in the back of her car. The call handler advised the calm mother to wake the child up, and when Louise did as instructed, she said the baby wasn't stirring. She couldn't get her out of her slumber. Louise suggested the youngster had stopped breathing, so an ambulance was sent out again.

For the second time in less than a month, paramedics had to tell Louise that her baby had passed away. The reaction was much the same as before - nothing. Cold, calm, quiet, and unbothered. Louise blamed the death on a bad bout of "flu."

It was also gathered that Scarlett hadn't just passed away; she'd been dead for some time before the call for "help" was made.

Where Louise had flown under the radar in Lexi's death, she wasn't able to evade scrutiny in Scarlett's death. It was just too coincidental; things didn't add up, and neither child had any preexisting conditions. For both to simply stop breathing weeks apart just didn't sit well with the police. They began to look into Louise Porton, and her twisted web of lies unraveled.

The night Scarlett passed away, Louise had taken her to stay in a nearby hotel. The reason for this overnight stay is unknown, but there was CCTV on the premises that caught Louise carrying her daughter out of the building, all bundled up in blankets, and placing her in the baby seat of her car. Louise said she was driving to the hospital to seek help for her unresponsive child. Still, on the way to the hospital, she stopped off for gas and parked up for a bit in a nearby parking lot. Here was where she made the 111 call.

Looking back, it's highly probable Scarlett was dead when Louise carried her out of the hotel building. The long drive to seek help was probably done so to make sure her baby had died. After all, she'd learned to wait before calling for help. The first two times she attempted to kill Lexi, she called for help too early, and paramedics were able to resuscitate the child. She knew if she waited a while, there was no chance of survival.

Forensics took the opportunity to investigate Scarlett's tiny body. She showed signs of her airways being intentionally blocked. As well as her neck being compressed, there were spatters of her blood on her pillow, a surefire sign of a smothering attempt. If this wasn't bad enough, when the police obtained Louise's phone records, they found some shocking internet searches. One read: *can you die if you have a blocked nose and cover your mouth with tape?*

Others questioned how long you need to wait after suffocation before you can no longer be resuscitated. There were also searches about drowning and how long it takes. We can only imagine the agony Louise potentially put her two younger children through before succeeding in her plan to end their lives.

She may have been caught far too late, especially considering she'd never tried to present herself as a caring mother, but the net had closed in on Louise. She was arrested but maintained her innocence. She had no reason or explanation for the disturbing searches she'd made around the time of the baby's deaths.

Her trial took place in August 2019, when Louise was 22 years old. Even while standing trial, she showed no signs of sorrow or remorse. While she couldn't explain away much of the prosecution's evidence against her, it felt as though Louise truly believed she was going to be let off the hook for this.

It was put to her that she found her babies to inconvenience her life, and Louise wanted to get rid of them so she could resume her sex work and party lifestyle without the hassle. Louise denied this and explained how she would accommodate her children's needs before her own. There was a plethora of evidence to rebuff this statement, however, including witnesses who saw the mother interact with her children or fob them off whenever she wanted to go out.

Every shred of evidence was put to Louise: the texts to meet men for sex while her daughter lay dead in hospital, her blasé number exchange with the hospital security guard, and the lack of grief in her messages just hours after Lexi died.

It was found there was no grief because Louise had been Lexi's murderer. There was no heartbreak when Scarlett died either - because she died at Louise's hands. She was found guilty in a unanimous verdict and given 32 years in jail. To this day, Louise Porton insists she's innocent.

This is a heartbreaking tale that also evokes much frustration. There are millions of women who have never been given the opportunity to have children despite their desperation to do so. Yet, here Louise Porton was, killing her two toddler girls just so she could resume her loose, carefree lifestyle. It's not like there wasn't any other way out - she didn't reach out to social services to say she was struggling with the ties of motherhood. She didn't call the police to confess she was thinking of hurting her babies. Her selfishness took the lives of two innocent babies, but thankfully, Louise never got the freedom she killed them for.

The Girl With Grit

Do you ever hear a noise as you lay in bed at night and wonder if you've locked the door? Do you freeze with anticipation while you listen out for a potential intruder in your kitchen, readying yourself for the attacker to make their way to you? When I lived alone, I certainly had my fair share of night time panic about these things. I even had a makeshift baseball bat my dad gave me to keep tucked beside my bedside table. Every unaccounted-for noise had me reaching for the bat. Part of me wanted to pull the sheets over my head until the threat went away; the other part of me made me get out of bed, bat in hand, to creep downstairs. I'd tremble in the cover of the shadows as I reached for the light switch.

It was always the dog scratching at the door to be let out or him chewing a marrowbone as loudly as he could. It was never an intruder. But, as this next tale shows, a stranger in the home - even in a highly secure, gated community - isn't that far-fetched.

Jennifer Morey was a 25-year-old woman who had spent the past few years dedicating herself to her career. The lawyer had put her head down and worked hard, which afforded her some promising career prospects and the ability to afford a place in a highly-secure apartment complex in an affluent area of Houston, Texas.

The young woman still found time to meet with friends despite her busy work schedule. This is just what she did on the night of April 14, 1995. She met up with a handful of girlfriends, had some drinks, and caught up on the latest gossip from the group. She'd had a fun night and let her hair down, which was much needed for Jennifer. Her job saw her work long hours, and she often took her work home, mentally at least.

Jennifer was spent after she said her goodbyes and retreated home for the night. Still, she maintained her night time routine: she took her contact lenses out, washed her face, moisturized, and brushed her teeth before she jumped into her cool, comfortable bed. She fell into a deep sleep. It could have been because of the alcohol or the copious amounts of dancing, but sleep came quickly for Jennifer.

Plus, she was comforted by the security of her apartment complex. Not only did it have an 8-foot fence surrounding the building, but also 24-hour security, with a guard on site all hours of the day. Still, in the early hours of April 15, Jennifer awoke to every woman's worst nightmare. There was a heavy weight on her that she quickly figured was a person. In her post-sleep haze, she tried to feel her way free but ended up grabbing the knife her attacker was holding to her neck.

Jennifer was jolted to the terrifying reality - this man was pulling at her underwear, and his intentions were clear.

Despite the fear Jennifer was feeling, she also felt shots of adrenaline pumping through her veins. If she could stop herself from being raped - one of the worst things that can happen to a woman, an irreversible experience - she was going to do it. Some women freeze in moments like this and choose to let the assailant do whatever they're going to do, hoping they'll be left alive at the end of it. Some women, like Jennifer, use the burst of adrenaline they feel to help them fight back. It's flight or fight in these instances, and Jennifer chose the latter.

This can sometimes work well, but it can also often get the victim in even hotter water. To anger the attacker is to possibly put themselves in even graver danger. Still, this was the route Jennifer took when she screamed and kicked and flailed as hard as she could. She wailed the apartment complex down, and over a dozen inhabitants heard Jennifer. You'd think this would have meant an urgent call to security was made; it wasn't. The other tenants tried to get back to sleep, perhaps kidding themselves; they'd just heard some wild animal noises or a catfight outside - not the desperate screams of a woman being attacked.

The screams angered the unknown man, who spat at his victim as he tried to cover her mouth, "Shut up, Jennifer!" He knew her name. She didn't think she recognized his voice, but he sure knew her. This stopped the shrieking woman for a moment as she tried to figure out if she could pinpoint the voice, but before she knew it, the attacker slashed at her face with his blade. He did so with such force Jennifer believed he'd taken her eye out with the knife. Blood pooled in the injured eye like a volcano, rendering her unable to see out of it. The man struck again and again. His attacks were ferocious, but the victim resumed her screaming.

The attacker retorted by slashing Jennifer's neck, not so much to incapacitate her, but enough to cause a rush of blood to spurt out. He was frighteningly close to her jugular, and had he slashed a few centimeters further, he'd have ended Jennifer's life there and then. Thankfully, he didn't, and despite the flow of blood dripping from her neck and eye, the victim didn't lose her will to live. She refused to allow him to sexually assault her. She would fight him to the death.

The attacker figured he was getting nowhere fighting the woman on her bed, so he got off her, pulled her bloodied body from the mattress, and dragged her into the bathroom. She wondered what his next move was going to be; why did he choose the bathroom? She could get more of a view of her attacker's silhouette now, but it was still just about pitch darkness. She noted his shortish hair and his medium build and tried to remember if she'd heard his voice before.

In the man's struggle to drag Jennifer to the bathroom, he dropped his weapon beside her bed. He left his victim in the bathtub and demanded she stay there as he retraced his steps to get his weapon. Jennifer had mere seconds to plan her next move: to fight him in the bathroom, where she was essentially cornered, or shut the door and try to stop him from getting in. The latter would be hard since the bathroom door didn't have a lock on it. Jennifer decided she would be the barrier behind the door, stopping her attacker from entering.

She jumped up from her crouched position in the bathtub, slammed the door between her and the violent intruder, and pushed her back against the door as hard as she could. She pushed her feet against the tub for leverage and mustered all of the strength within her. She would not let this man win - no way, no how.

Most men are stronger than women. Even if a man and woman are the same size, there is often a disparity in strength. The attacker had brute force on his side, and he made an attempt to beat the door down. Defiant Jennifer would have to be immobile to allow her relentless attacker from snaring her. The stress hormones surging around Jennifer's shaky body were the only thing keeping her going. She could see her blood dripping from her face and neck to her torso and pooling on the floor. She knew she would bleed to death if she didn't get help soon.

Suddenly, the banging stopped. It was eerily quiet. From the deafening banging to now being able to hear a pin drop, Jennifer tried to hold on, pushing against the bath while listening for her attacker. She pressed her head against the door, trying to make out what the violent man was doing in her apartment. He was shuffling around, but she could hear he was no longer right outside the door.

Jennifer took this opportunity to reach over to the toilet roll so she could press it against her neck. It was a brave move, considering she was the only thing stopping her attacker from barging through the door. She swiped the roll from its holder and pressed the paper to the wide slice across her neck. She knew she didn't have long before she passed out and eventually bled out.

Then, as she was considering her next move, she heard the man pull his zipper up on his pants. After that, there was no more noise. No more shuffling or rustling around in her things. It was now or never - Jennifer had to make a break for it, or she'd die alone on her cold bathroom floor. There was a chance her attacker was tricking her and was still outside, but this was a fight the defiant woman was willing to take on. She wasn't going to make it by simply staying put.

She wrapped her hands around the metal door handle. Her fingers were wet with blood, making it near impossible for her to get a grip and pull the door open. She tried again - her hands just slipped right off, almost as if she was putting no effort in at all, like the handle was made of melting ice. Not only that, she'd managed to lock herself in by jamming the door so hard that it was wedged tightly shut. She'd pushed so hard that the door was stuck.

Jennifer didn't come this far to only come this far, though. It would have been a tragic irony that she'd survived a horrific attack only to have locked herself in the bathroom and bleed to death there.

With a lot of grit and frustration, Jennifer finally yanked the door open. She reached up to the wall and found the light switch. She flicked it, but nothing happened. It was still pitch dark. She crawled on the floor to another light switch, but again, no light came. Aware the man might still be there, she knew she needed to remain quiet and in the shadows. There was hope he couldn't see her if she couldn't see him.

She blindly reached her landline and pulled it to her ear. There was no tone. It was dead. The power had been cut. This had been planned by the attacker; that much became clear to Jennifer.

It was 1995; people just didn't have cell phones like they do now. Jennifer was one of the few who'd acquired the new technology, and she pulled it from her drawer and dialed 911. "This guy just tried to cut my throat." the exasperated woman told the handler. The man on the other end of the line picked up on Jennifer's fragile frame of mind straight away. It seems the woman may have still believed her attacker was tricking her and questioned the handler about his name. "My name is Richard," he told her and advised her to calm down and stay on the line.

"I'm sorry," Jennifer said. "I'm calming down."

Richard did a great job of bringing Jennifer down to a less inflamed state, talking to her while the officers were on their way to her apartment. Then, a sudden banging on her front door made her jump, almost dropping the large cell phone from her hands. It must be the officers, Jennifer thought and headed to answer.

"Don't answer the door," Richard warned her.

"It's security; I'm here to help," the man behind the door promised. Still, Richard was urging the bloodied woman not to open the door. Richard said the police weren't close to her apartment yet; he could see their location on the GPS tracker. "But he said he's going to help me," Jennifer reasoned. "Do not answer the door if you don't know the man - look through the peephole," he urged the woman. Jennifer didn't know the man, and he wasn't wearing the security hat the guards usually wore. She refused to answer.

There wasn't much more of a wait until the police arrived. Richard gave confirmation it really was the police at the door, so Jennifer unlocked it as instructed. She was rushed to the hospital to have her potentially fatal wounds seen. It wouldn't be long before the culprit was found, either. In fact, he'd identified himself when he knocked on her door: 26-year-old Bryan Wayne Gibson, the on-site guard at her complex. He left his security hat inside her apartment while carrying out his vicious attack on the woman and must have realized part way back to his post. Should Jennifer have opened the door to him, it's highly likely she'd not have survived the night.

When Jennifer awoke from surgery, she was greeted by the police officers who tended to the crime scene. "You put up one hell of a fight," they told her. They also informed her of the identity of her attacker. Shivers went down Jennifer's spine: the very person who ought to have offered protection was the man who'd tried to kill her. He was paid to ensure the resident's safety; instead, he felt it appropriate to try and rape and murder them. Thanks to Jennifer's strength of character, he never got the chance to do either of those things.

Gibson didn't admit to the attack despite the huge amount of evidence that placed him inside Jennifer's apartment that night. His underwear was picked up from her bedroom floor. His security hat was strewn on the floor. He'd also left one stray glove and his belt. Not only that, his knife was recovered, too. It seems like he left just about all of his belongings in Jennifer's apartment, which helped justice be served.

Still, Gibson insisted he was attacked by the man who tried to kill Jennifer - he had wounds to prove it. These wounds, however, were consistent with defensive strikes from Jennifer, not a random attacker.

It's hard to say Gibson's employers had no clue about his inappropriate behavior at work. He had been reassigned to various apartment complexes due to client complaints about his behavior. Instead of being fired or spoken to by his employer, they just kept moving this problem employee from one job to another. Had they tackled him head-on, it's unlikely he'd have had the opportunity to break into Jennifer's and try to take her life.

It's interesting to know that the company that employed Gibson had over 100 of its employees convicted of crimes in just four years, between 1991 and 1994. It seems Gibson was one of many with criminal urges, although it's down to speculation as to why the company managed to have so many felons on its payroll.

Bryan Wayne Gibson's tall tale wasn't believed by the judge at his trial, who handed him 20 years behind bars for attempted murder.

As with all traumatic events, they take some time to get over. It took Jennifer a while to get back on her feet. As you can imagine, living in her apartment was no longer an option. She only revisited the crime scene once - to pick up her stuff and get out of there as fast as she could.

Jennifer's confidence hit rock bottom, as did her trust in people. Sadly, so did her trust in herself. She had an unsteady work life for a while, and it seemed like all the years of hard work she'd put into becoming a lawyer were slowly being poured down the drain. She took on jobs she was wildly over-experienced for. She floundered in junior roles despite her wealth of knowledge.

Where there is darkness, there must be light. For Jennifer, it took years, but the light finally appeared when she got some closure. In 1998, the company that employed Gibson as her apartment's security awarded Jennifer an undisclosed sum of money to compensate her. This helped her open her own law practice in Fort Worth, Texas. They say good things come in threes, and she would soon after meet the man who became her husband.

A sweet aspect of an otherwise terrifying case is that Jennifer and Richard - the call handler who took her panicked 911 call - are close friends to this day. She commends his comforting words and the life-saving advice he gave her: *don't open the door*. Richard even attended her wedding - one that may not have taken place had Richard not been on the other end of the phone that day.

Hunger For Depravity

I vividly remember being around six or seven years old and my dad putting a VHS on of a horror movie - I don't recall the name, but I sure recall the sickening feeling it gave me. The plot and actors in the movie escape me; all I can remember is how disgusted I was by one particular scene. The scene involved cannibalism, brains specifically, and as I watched in shock, I suddenly went off the plate of lasagne on my lap. I got in trouble for not eating my dinner that evening, but I couldn't explain why - I just knew that the film (highly inappropriate for my age, but that's another story) made me want to puke.

Cannibalism evokes a similar response in me to this day. I find the act of one human eating another vomit-inducing. I don't particularly like reading or hearing about it, much less seeing graphic depictions of it.

Still, this chapter is all about Armin Meiwes and his cannibalistic ways. I'm still unsure why I chose to cover a case that's going to make me wince the whole time I write it; regardless, I've committed, so here we go.

Armin Meiwes was born in December 1961 in Kassel, Germany, which is famed for its World Heritage Park and impressive historical buildings. By all accounts, Armin lived a life of solitude as a child. With few friends and a father who was indifferent to him, the boy struggled socially. All he had were his toys and imagination. He liked stories and fairytales, particularly the tale of Hansel and Gretel. As children, we all have that one story or fable that resonates with us. For me, Rumpelstiltskin frightened the life out of me. So much so that the picture book I had of the tale was securely hidden at the bottom of my toybox. Still, I would talk about it to my grandparents, asking why the imp wanted a newborn, why did the girl only get three guesses, and *who's called Rumpelstiltskin anyway*?

It was a morbid fascination born out of fear. For Armin, his fascination with Hansel and Gretel was with one particular scene where the witch intends to fatten Hansel up in order to eat him. He would, by his father's accounts, obsess over this part of the story, talking about it relentlessly.

Armin's loneliness was further compounded when, at age eight, his father left the family unit. He wouldn't have any regular contact with his dad after this, resulting in the boy desperate for a father figure in his life. He still had his mother, but she became overbearing and suppressive. She would scold him in front of other people, embarrass him, and insist on chaperoning him everywhere, even as he entered his teens.

With no solid father figure in his life, Armin made his own up, an imaginary brother. It was to this pretend sibling he would confess his cannibalistic feelings; he wanted to eat his schoolmates. Not in a violent, animalistic way, but so these children would live on within Armin and keep him company forever. They couldn't abandon him if he ate them, and he'd never be lonely again.

It was clear the boy was troubled by his loneliness, but Armin's mother didn't do anything to remedy this. She felt all her son needed was her, and that's how it was until 1999 when she died. Armin was still living with his mother, almost 40, with no significant other in sight. Naturally, Armin was devastated by his mother's passing, but there was no denying she was an overbearing and controlling part of Armin's life. He'd known no different - until now.

For the first time in his life, he could explore his own interests and hobbies without input - or put-downs - from his mother. Still, he was left alone in the big family home, and to fill the gap his mother left, he created a shrine for her. Pictures, personal items, and even a mannequin that resembled his late mother were neatly assembled in Armin's tribute room. It seems Armin humanized the plastic dummy, as when the sun went down, he laid the figure down on a pillow as if it were going to go to sleep.

With his mother now out of his life, Armin was free to thoroughly explore all of the burning desires he'd been suppressing all these years, specifically searching out torture on the internet. These shocking videos and pictures didn't shock or disgust the man - he would view them regularly as a source of pleasure.

This depraved interest led him to online chat rooms dedicated to cannibalism. Here, he'd have intense conversations with others interested in the twisted act. The year after his mother's death, in 2000, Armin put out an advert on the chat site. He was searching for a man, specifically between the ages of 18 and 30. Ideally, the man would be well-built and have a strong desire to be eaten. Surprisingly, Armin had a number of responses to this advertisement, but he chose Borg Jose, who seemed to fit the bill better than all other applicants.

As they'd planned, Borg made his way to Armin's home and was tied up on the kitchen table, ready to be cut apart. Suddenly, though, Borg had a change of heart. He felt ill; he no longer wanted to proceed. What was once a fantasy had suddenly become a reality for the man, and he didn't like it one bit. Armin set the man free and let him go.

Armin revisited his list of potential men. Another one that stuck out was 43-year-old Bernd-Jürgen Brandes. Sure, he was over a decade older than the age he desired the victim to be, but beggars couldn't be choosers. The rest of the applicants didn't quite meet the rest of Armin's criteria, so he chose Brandes to be his second chance at eating another human. The pair exchanged emails and deeply discussed their plans to eat and be eaten. One of Armin's suggestions was that he would use his new friend's skull as a makeshift ashtray after he'd consumed him.

The friendship developed into something more, and in March 2001, the pair met up at Armin's home. They got intimate, but that wasn't the only reason Brandes made the visit. He wanted to be cooked and eaten. He was even planning on consuming some of his own flesh.

In preparation for this, Brandes took handfuls of sleeping tablets in preparation for having his genitals cut off and eaten. To help him deal with the pain of the procedure - which I can only imagine as being agonizing - he also downed alcohol and cough medicine, although I'm not sure how effective this would've been in quelling the pain he was in. Armin set up a video camera to capture the whole thing.

Armin and Brandes agreed the time was right to begin. With the camera rolling, Armin took a knife and began sawing at his willing victim's intimate area. Prior to this - and this fact truly makes me wince - he'd tried biting it off. It was an unsuccessful attempt that caused the cannibal to reach for a knife to do the bloody job.

Once it was removed, the two men sat and ate the raw flesh. However, they discovered that the "meat" (as they viewed it) was too chewy to fully consume, so Armin unleashed his inner chef by heating a pan with oil, salt, pepper, garlic, and red wine before carefully placing the flesh on the scolding pan. Armin was too distracted to keep an eye on the sizzling frying pan and accidentally burned their supper. This rendered their intended food indelible.

Meanwhile, as you can imagine, Brandes was losing a lot of blood. There was no chance the man was going to make it out of this alive, and he knew this. It was too late to back out now, even if he wanted to; he was in no fit state. He was drifting in and out of consciousness, although still willing to try and consume some of his own flesh. Armin decided to run a warm bath and place the dying man there, perhaps believing he'd have a more comfortable exit in the water.

While Brandes lay in the bath, Armin opened a book and distracted himself from the man's slow death in his bathroom. He would close the science fiction book every 15 minutes or so and make his way to the bathroom to check on Brandes. He did this multiple times but was getting agitated that his companion seemed to be suffering a prolonged death. To put him out of his agony, Armin decided to grab a knife from the kitchen and stab Brandes in the throat multiple times. The willing victim - such a strange phrase to use, and not one I'm overly comfortable using - was now dead.

This wouldn't be the end of Armin's cannibalistic acts, though. In fact, it was just the beginning. He lifted the dead body from the bathtub and carried him to a meat hook he'd installed for this moment. He hung the body up - all of this caught on the camera Armin had set up - and began to butcher the deceased man.

Armin dismembered the man and stored his chunks of flesh in his freezer for later consumption. The body parts lasted over ten months - Armin had consumed a total of 44 lbs of Brandes.

The following winter, the cannibal found his supply was running low. Nothing had come of his involvement in Brandes death, so the man felt confident enough to head back to his cannibalism chat room and recruit a new victim. Again, he placed an ad for someone - a young man - to come to his home and be willingly eaten by him.

Not everyone on the site was into cannibalism - sure, they'd taken a look out of morbid curiosity, perhaps. But they'd never partake in such a thing, much less stand by while some man on the internet was recruiting (possibly) vulnerable men to cook and eat. It just so happens an Austrian man was perusing the chat site around the time Armin posted his second ad. Sickened by the discovery, he went straight to the police with this information.

Armin had revealed enough information about himself on the internet for authorities to know exactly who - and where - he was. At the beginning of December 2002, they burst into his home and arrested him. During the raid, they searched his property, and the tip-off they'd received from the Austrian man was true. There were human remains in the freezer. Just as incriminating was a VHS tape that was recovered. It showed in bloody detail Armin placing Brandes on a meat hook and butchering his body.

It took eight months for the man to be charged with murder. Authorities took their time to gather evidence for the case, which wasn't as clear-cut as initially thought. While Armin had indeed killed a man and subsequently eaten him, the man was a willing participant in this. Investigators had to comb through Armin's internet history, viewing his hundreds of cannibalism chats and view his plethora of images depicting torture.

The issue here was, if your victim is a willing party in their murder, is it still murder? Is the person still a victim? Is this still a crime in the eyes of the law? A gray area was the legality of cannibalism in Germany. Technically, it's not illegal. Immoral, of course, but illegal, no. This was another barrier prosecutors found themselves running into.

By the end of January 2004, it was decided: Armin Meiwes was guilty of manslaughter and handed eight and a half years in jail. This caused an outcry of anger from the German public. It was beyond lenient, they said and demanded a heftier form of justice. A retrial was agreed to, which took place in 2006. The disturbing case was looked at from a completely new angle.

The initial trial suggested Armin killed Brandes because that's what the victim asked him to do. This may have been the case, but it was argued that the true motive behind the murder was to satisfy the culprit's sexual desires. They also noted that Brandes was so far gone due to the sleeping pills and alcohol he consumed prior to his participation in the cannibalism he had no way to express any desire to back out of his own murder.

In the spring of 2006, Armin's sentence was extended. Now, he was given life behind bars.

While in jail, the killer became a vegetarian.

Evil Among Us

The thing about likable, upstanding community members is that nobody would ever suspect them of wrongdoing. They're helpful, always say hello when they pass you in the street, and don't act vexed when your child keeps accidentally throwing their ball in their yard. As a whole, you view them as trustworthy, calm, and reliable individuals. The terrifying thing is psychopaths can often mimic this behavior, and we can rarely tell.

Murderers in the suburbs - the ones with tight family units, well-paying jobs, bustling social lives, and close spouses - have me questioning my own judgment of people. All too often, we're convinced by TV shows and movies that killers are easy to spot. They're creepy, dress like they don't have access to a washing machine, and have poor social skills. If only this were true, we could pinpoint them a mile off. This case is a stark reminder of how anyone can be harboring dark thoughts, no matter their social status. More than that, upstanding members of our society can also be capable of carrying out vicious killings before coming home and acting perfectly normal.

Trent Benson was born in October 1971 in South Korea. Little is known about his birth parents since they abandoned the boy in a cruel way. He was left to his own devices on the streets and was discovered wandering by an orphanage that took him in. He was three years old at this point, but you can imagine his first few years in the world were filled with neglect and possibly abuse. Still, this would change when David and Elizabeth Benson contacted the orphanage and expressed their interest in bringing the boy over to America.

Sure enough, the youngster was brought into the Benson family unit, who resided in Fosston, Minnesota. The Bensons were used to the adoption process and taking in children with extra emotional needs since they'd gone through the process multiple times before. By the time Trent got there, he had several adopted siblings who'd welcome him into his new, loving home.

The Benson's lived for their kids. They were a well-rounded couple who parented with patience and empathy and made sure their kids wanted absolutely nothing. They didn't spoil the children - as much as they wanted to - but they always had everything they needed. It seemed little Trent's poor start in life hadn't done any lasting emotional damage to the boy since he was a clever student and a gifted young sportsman.

These attributes flourished in high school, where he ended up captaining the swimming team. He was well-liked by his peers, too, and could be described as the type of kid who got on with everyone. He didn't subscribe to one friendship group or clique but rather treated everybody the same. He was inoffensive, kind, and above average in his grades.

However, as he journeyed further into his teens, a dark side began to emerge. At the time, it probably wasn't viewed as anything sinister, but in hindsight, we can see Trent's adolescent acts were troubling. After leaving high school, Trent was arrested for shoplifting from a department store. There was no reason for this other than the desire to get away with it. He wasn't short on money and could have afforded the item he tried to steal. He was arrested for this attempted thievery.

In 1990, Trent went on to study at Minnesota State University Moorhead, where he exhibited some red-flag behavior. He'd begun to take a keen interest in the opposite sex by this point, although the manner in which he pursued them was questioned by some of his peers.

He would be persistent, show anger or frustration if he didn't get what he wanted from girls he liked, and would reveal a darker side to prospective love interests.

Only a few of his classmates would see this behavior, though, and the others would be blind to his sinister capabilities. Trent was able to maintain his "nice guy" image despite his dating indiscretions at university, with his friends describing him as passive, easygoing, and a generally good-natured guy.

Graduation came quickly, and Trent was thrust into the real world. He would gain odd jobs in his home state of Minnesota but would move to Mesa, Arizona, in 1996, where he found work at a car dealership. Trent set up a home in Mesa, meeting a woman he would quickly marry. They had a son together, and it seemed as if the young family were a happy unit, to the outside at least. Trent would soon become unhappy within the relationship, however. He filed for divorce a few years after their nuptials, noting that his former wife's drinking had driven him to leave her.

By now, it was 2000, and Trent's parents funded the purchase of a condominium for him in Mesa. If you lived alongside Trent, he was the type of neighbor you hope and pray for: one who respects your privacy, doesn't bother you with loud music and offers a helping hand if you need one. He would be an integral member of the homeowner's association, causing Trent to become a highly respected member of the affluent community. The only thing Trent didn't have that most of his neighbors did was the brag-worthy job. His parents again stepped in and rectified this by buying him a space in the local mall, where the man would set up a shop to sell various goods, including ice cream.

Trent was young, free, and single and would frequent strip clubs when he wasn't working or maintaining his property. On a cool November night, Trent spent a few hours at a club he was a regular at. The drive home saw him spot a sex worker, 21-year-old Alisa Marie Beck, who he picked up.

Trent handed the woman her payment once they were done, but something got him enraged before she managed to get out of his vehicle. It's been suggested that she made offensive statements regarding his sexual conduct; that she laughed at him, and this made him enraged. Whether or not this is true, only two people truly know the answer to that, and one of them met a grizzly end that night.

The rage-filled man grabbed Alisa's head from behind and slammed it as hard as he could into the steering wheel, taking out all of his anger on the helpless woman, who was being knocked senseless by her client. Trent then put both hands around the young woman's neck and choked the life out of her. He flung her out of his car, half-naked, into a dirt-filled alleyway for her to be found just hours later.

There was a quiet period for Trent, where he seemingly didn't unleash his inner rage for another three years. In late 2007, he would strike again, this time with much more force than his initial crime. It's not ascertained if Trent picked up his first victim with the intent of harming her. But, this time, there's no question as to what the violent man's intent was when he bundled a 47-year-old woman off the street into his car.

Once at a derelict house, he forced the woman inside and began aggressively pulling her clothing from her. She knew what was about to happen and was powerless to stop it. Trent was by no means big in stature, but he was capable of overpowering every victim unlucky enough to encounter him.

He raped the woman before fleeing back to his Sedan and driving off. The inconsolable woman was left in an area she was unfamiliar with, so she stumbled from the abandoned house and walked the streets in search of some help. By a stroke of luck, a taxi was driving past, and the traumatized woman made her way toward it. She didn't ask to be taken to the hospital or the police station but went home instead. Once in the comfort of her own place, she found the courage to contact the police, and she made a report.

Later that year, in October 2007, Trent headed off in search of a sex worker to pick up. Eventually, he found Karen Campell, a 44-year-old woman who was standing alone on a dimly lit street, and pulled up beside her. The pair spoke after Trent wound his vehicle window down and spent a few minutes negotiating a price they were both happy with. It's uncertain why Trent entered negotiations here since he would go on to brutally murder the woman. Surely the price didn't matter, although maybe he was simply trying to act like a normal client.

After the exchange, Trent slaughtered the woman by unknown means. It's never been released to the public just how the killer ended his victim's life, but it was explained by police as being particularly barbaric. After the violent assault on the woman, Trent discarded her body on a side street but left part of her body on the main sidewalk. In doing so, he unintentionally ran over the naked woman in his haste to flee the murder scene. Despite Trent's lousy attempt at concealing the body, it took ten whole days for Karen to be found. At this point, the police hadn't pieced together that there was a serial sex attacker/murderer on the loose.

His crimes were getting closer together, though. The rush of the kills and the relief of getting away with them seemed to fuel Trent's ego. He knew he'd pulled the wool over people's eyes and that his local community thought he was a shining example of a perfect neighbor. In reality, the man was spiraling into a persistent rage that he'd take out on unsuspecting sex workers.

He'd take another victim less than a month later, in November 2007. This time, though, he swapped locations and swapped Mesa for Phoenix. It could be that Trent wanted to throw police off the scent of him - not that they had one - by mixing up his murderous playgrounds.

The serial offender scoured the streets, looking for his newest prey. Eventually, he discovered a 35-year-old woman he followed for a while before forcing her into his vehicle. He locked her inside and drove to another abandoned house he was aware of and pummeled her as he dragged her inside. The beating continued once the pair were inside, where Trent also raped the hysterical victim. By some miracle, the woman survived the attack. The beating she received was violent and could have been fatal if the attacker had done a fraction more damage.

Again, once he was done, the barbaric serial sex offender fled the scene. The woman, when she was able to drag herself from her bloody slumber, managed to find her way outside, where a member of the public spotted her and got her to safety. Another police report was quickly filed.

Meanwhile, Trent resumed his life as a stand-up guy. He basked in his position as a well-respected member of the community, a reliable local business owner, and a devoted dad. How could anyone know the truth? He hid his twisted predilections so well.

None of his Mesa community knew Trent had prior run-ins with the law over his use of sex workers. Sex work is not legal in Arizona, but Trent's use of such workers was well-known to officials. Still, it took them a hot minute to put the dots together since the spate of sex attacks wasn't considered to be connected initially.

To confirm this assumption, they cross-referenced the DNA the attacker left on his victims. Sure enough, it was the same guy committing all of the incredibly similar attacks. However, the DNA didn't match any they already had in their systems. Whoever was doing this wasn't a known offender, which frustrated the investigators. They decided the culprit was clearly a frequent client of sex workers and made a list of those known to them for engaging in sexual services. One of the first names that interested them was Trent's. They didn't think bringing him in for question would do anything, much less convince him to offer up a sample of his DNA.

Investigators had to be clever. They began surveilling him, keeping a close eye on his movements. They were searching for something they could take his DNA from: a piece of discarded gum, a plastic beer cup he'd been using - anything that could tie him to the crimes.

It was an arduous, painstaking task, but one that needed to be carried out. Police needed to either exclude him from their inquiries or capture him. Eventually, the investigator tailing Trent followed him after he discarded his cigarette and picked the butt up from the floor. *Jackpot*, he thought, as he bagged it, sealed it, and sent it to forensics.

Sure enough, Trent Benson was the man they were after. Trent was arrested on the afternoon of May 14, 2008, and taken to Mesa Police Department for questioning.

His arrest was on the local news, and the community couldn't believe what they were seeing. Not passive, affable Trent? He's not capable of such violence or brutality. The sickening news trickled its way back to Minnesota, too, where Trent's old friends were equally as shocked by the arrest. Many believed it to be a case of wrongful arrest or mistaken identity. Some, particularly the girls Trent aggressively pursued in university, weren't so surprised at the news.

When cases like this come to light, you often hear of the ex-wife or ex-partner coming forward to share that the accused was, in fact, abusive towards them, too. All too often, the former partners had been keeping their ex's violence a secret until they had no choice but to expose them. This wasn't one of those cases. Just like many of Trent's friends and family, she too was shocked that her ex-husband could be capable of such horrific rapes and murders. She was in disbelief that her docile ex and the father of her child had committed these crimes.

The police's work wasn't done just yet, though. There was another unsolved murder of a sex worker in Mesa in 2007. Elisa Dewakuku had been found half-naked in a canal, having been strangled to death. Trent didn't deny having used the woman for her services and even went as far as to admit he got violent with the woman. He stopped short of admitting to her murder, though. He said he couldn't remember the rest of the evening after he began beating the woman.

Investigators had a hunch the serial sex offender wasn't working alone. They thought another man had been involved in at least some of the attacks, but the theory hasn't been proven, nor has any evidence to support this been brought forward.

Trent's trial took place in 2011. It took so long to go from his arrest to trial because his defense was trying to gather information on his early life prior to being adopted by the Bensons. It was their hope they'd explain away their client's clearly indefensible violence and sexual aggression by blaming it on his childhood. This tactic proved to be futile, however, since Trent was found guilty of four rapes and two murders and handed the death penalty.

It's worth noting that the police believe there to be more victims of Trent Benson who haven't been - or are yet to be - discovered. This seems likely, particularly since sex workers in 90s Mesa were often transients with little in the way of family and friends. Still, the killer has made no more admissions since his 2011 sentencing and remains on death row today.

She Killed To See What It Felt Like

Intrusive thoughts are something I think many of us have dealt with over the years. For those of you lucky enough not to know what one of these is, it's an unpleasant involuntary thought, often a violent one. It leaves our head as quickly as it enters, but we're left thinking about the upsetting image for hours - or days - afterward. Some people have these thoughts about someone else being hurt; others have thoughts of themselves carrying out an act of violence.

When I first heard about this crime, I did wonder if the killer in this case had endured one of these nasty thoughts and done the unthinkable - carried it out. Nothing added up; why did this murder happen? Why was the killer hysterical after they'd done it? The more I looked into it, the less I could explain how this crime came to fruition. Lindsay Haugen and her boyfriend, Robby Mast, had been happy in the short time they'd been together. Even on the day she killed him.

Lindsay had a troubled youth. Like a lot of teens, she rebelled and experimented with drugs and alcohol. However, her experience with drugs didn't end up being a fleeting phase - she ran away from home at the age of 15 and was addicted to heroin by 16. With no stability or guidance, the wayward teen soon fell pregnant.

When she discovered she was going to be a mother, she made her way back to her family home. Her mother agreed to take care of the child, allowing Haugan to join the National Guard, a time when she has described herself as being happy. During this time, she fell in love with a man - but it wouldn't be the happy ending she'd dreamed of.

Her lover was abusive. He not only beat her violently - so much so he broke her nose and hand on different occasions - he was also sexually abusive. The relationship offered little in the way of stability or comfort for Lindsay, who stuck it out as long as she could. Eventually, with nowhere to turn for help except the authorities, the woman did what she had to do to get the violent man out of her life. She didn't want to turn him in, but knew she'd wind up dead if she didn't escape.

In the summer of 2015, her ex was sent to jail for the two years of abuse he'd inflicted upon her. Finally, Lindsay was free. She had to quit her post in the National Guard, however, to fully cut ties with that nightmarish chapter of her life.

It wouldn't be long before she embarked on a new relationship when she met Robby Mast at a friend's house party. The pair got talking and hit it off straight away.

Floridian Robby was born in 1990 and was brought up by his mother, Dori. He didn't have much of a relationship with his father but was close to his stepfather, Gene. The typical 9-5 lifestyle had never interested Robby. He felt there was more to life than being chained to a desk or chasing money. He didn't know what was missing in his life but he knew there was something. So, in 2008, when he was 18, he took off from the comfort of his childhood home and traveled the country.

He took rides on trains, bikes, cars, and buses, often hitchhiking his way from one state to another, enjoying his transient way of living. He'd take jobs here and there to sustain himself but would often find himself drawn into using drugs and alcohol to fill a void he had. He was constantly fleeing from one city to another in search of something to take away his sadness.

It seemed he'd found it in August 2015 when he met Lindsay. So much so that when the woman suggested joining Robby on his travels, he agreed she should come. She'd just escaped a horrible time in her life and decided an adventure was just what she needed. Robby quickly began telling Lindsay about his depression, going as far as expressing his desire to die.

Lindsay wasn't sure if he was serious about it. She felt upset that he was in such a dark place, and despite her attempts at trying to comfort him, Robby still spoke of his wish to die.

The pair had traveled together for a month, and in that time, Robby went from talking of death to outright asking Lindsay to kill him. Again, she wasn't sure if her lover was having an especially bad day or was being serious. It became apparent that, when he was asking frequently for her to kill him, he was truly serious.

The more she noticed Robby in pain, the more she considered ending his clear misery. Eventually, when the man made another request for his girlfriend to kill him, he got the response she thought he was looking for: "If you really want that, I can make it happen." Robby said it was what he wanted.

By this point in the night, the young couple had been drinking in their truck, sharing bottles of wine and a takeaway pizza. Could it have been the drink talking for Robby?

There'd be no chance to find out since Lindsay took herself to the back seat, right behind where Robby was sitting in the front. She slipped her arms through to the front and put her boyfriend in a tight chokehold, although Lindasy would say she didn't really think she was doing it tight enough. Still, she admitted to squeezing her partner's neck and recalled how he had a moment of shaking. She thought he was waking from his slumber and was going to stop her, although she still maintained the grip on his neck.

Eventually, the woman released her arms and let Robby go. He slumped in the chair. Panic set in for Lindsay, the reality of what she'd just done hitting her like a ton of bricks. She didn't want him to die, nor did she want to get in trouble for murder - although she had always wanted to know how it felt to kill someone. Specifically, Lindsay had been interested in what it would feel like to end someone's life with your bare hands. Now, she was confronted with this prospect.

This type of thought, for me, can often be branded as an intrusive thought. Macabre, violent thoughts that aren't really our own, something we would be disgusted by even thinking of, let alone carrying out. In this case, though, it seems Lindsay truly did harbor the desire to know the feeling of being a murderer.

While in a panic, Lindsay tried to perform CPR on the young man, to no avail. In her post-murder haze, she buckled her victim in his seat while he foamed at the mouth. People began to see the drunken woman acting strangely, so police were called to the parking lot. When officers arrived, they found Lindsay in a frantic state and her boyfriend in the front seat dead. She was immediately arrested and admitted culpability - to a point, at least.

She said she tried to release her grip, but Robby kept pulling her arms forward to resume her hold on his neck. This was brushed off as lies by investigators, who said this was an impossibility. How could an unconscious man keep lifting his arms to help his attacker continue choking him?

In the spring of 2016, the trial commenced, and Lindsay was given 60 years behind bars for deliberate homicide. She can, however, apply for parole after serving a quarter of this sentence.

There is also another perplexing aspect to this case. Robby's mother and stepfather wrote a letter to Lindsay to tell her they forgave her for murdering their son. She replied to them, which caused a back-and-forth exchange between the parents and the convict.

After a while, they agreed it would be better to meet Lindsay in person, which they did. One visit turned into two, and Lindsay quickly began to develop a bond with Dori and Gene. They'd talk about Robby, about her life in prison, and they'd pray together. As Gene put it, he may have lost a son, but he gained a daughter.

Many of us just can't imagine reacting this way if someone stripped us of our child, but the parents insist it was the only way. The religious couple felt that if they offered her forgiveness, God would, too. They set about helping the young woman find faith in order to save her from her sins. They're bigger people that I believe would be in the same situation. Still, I know forgiveness can offer the victims of crimes peace from the feelings of anger and bitterness that would otherwise plague them.

Better Late Than Never

As I mentioned at the beginning of this book, true crime followers seek justice in every case we encounter. Ideally, it's right after they've committed their crime, so they don't have the opportunity to remain on the streets and cause pain and anguish to anybody else. But we don't live in a world that accommodates our desire for justice, much less immediate justice.

Still, when someone is apprehended for crimes they committed decades earlier, it's still a win for those of us who despise violent offenders - a criminal is still being made to face up to their abhorrent acts. Of course, we'd prefer that the felon didn't get years of freedom, but the alternative - that they'd remained free their whole lives - is an unimaginable scenario. We'll take these wins where we get them.

The case of David Thomas Boyd is one such case. The violent man was able to get away with atrocities for far, far too long. How someone can live with the knowledge of vile deeds they'd done years earlier baffles me. I don't mean things like saying cruel things to your mom or lying as a teenager - I mean truly unforgivable things, like child murder. I have no clue how perpetrators of such crimes, who seemingly got away with them, are able to sleep easily at night. Do their crimes not haunt them in their dreams? Does their evil wrongdoing catch up with them the older they get? Or aren't they capable of remorse and feelings of guilt? Don't they care about the evil they've committed?

In this case, as far as I can tell, it's the latter.

In the early 90s, kids were granted greater freedom than the children of today. We were allowed to explore the nearby woods to take ourselves to the store with our pocket money, and our curfew was signaled when the sun was going down. There was no safety net of mobile phones or their tracking apps. Parents of today often act shocked at the level of freedom we were given back then, considering the fact the dangers of strangers were still drilled into us.

In early October 1992, little Nikki Allan was visiting her granddad's flat in Sunderland, U.K. The seven-year-old was streetsmart and was granted the freedom to make her way from her home to her granddad's as she pleased. After all, it wasn't far away at all, and the young girl was familiar with the area and its residents.

On this particular day, Nikki had spent the early evening with her grandparent but noticed the streetlights outside had come on. This was the sign she needed that it was hometime and that she would be expected home any minute now. It was around 8:30 pm when Nikki gave her granddad a hug goodbye and made her way out of his home to skip her way up the street to the home she shared with her mother, stepdad, and two younger siblings.

Nikki's upbringing was modest but filled with love. She was the apple of her granddad's eye, and the feeling was reciprocated. She loved nothing more than spending time with him, watching TV in his flat. Unbeknown to the doting grandparent, October 7 would be the last time he'd see his granddaughter alive.

On this fateful day, she was taken from the family who adored her by a wicked man who spotted her as she was making her way home. The man followed the child and managed to strike up a conversation. Nikki was a friendly little girl, but like every other seven-year-old in the area, she had been warned to stay away from strangers.

Meanwhile, Sharon Henderson, Nikki's mother, was just getting home and expected to see her little girl in her pajamas sitting in the living room, waiting to say goodnight. However, the little girl wasn't home. Despite her young age, she was usually a good timekeeper. The initial worry soon turned into panic when she discovered her daughter had left her granddads to make her way home. Something - or someone - had stopped that from happening.

Sharon called upon the local community, knocking on doors to see if the neighbors had seen her daughter in the past few hours. None of them had seen the girl, but they all grabbed their coats and headed out to help Sharon search for the child. By now, it was dark. The only thing guiding their search was the orange hues from the street lamps above, so getting a good look down alleyways and behind bushes proved difficult.

There was no sign of the girl, and eventually, the search party had to retreat until the following day.

When daylight broke the morning after Nikki's disappearance, the search resumed, and it wasn't long before a heartbreaking discovery was made. Her tiny shoes and winter coat were found discarded outside of a derelict building close to the nearby city center. The Quayside Old Exchange hadn't been tended to for some time; its only inhabitants were pigeons and rats. Naturally, the search took them inside the rubble-filled building, and after a thorough forage through the debris, they discovered the young girl lying dead in the basement.

Her death was no accident. She'd been stabbed almost 40 times. Nikki's head had been bludgeoned by a nearby brick. Dried blood covered her body. The worst possible case scenario had been realized. Heartbroken, Sharon had to break the news to Nikki's granddad, whose world collapsed around him. The bereft mother didn't allow herself much time to grieve since her emptiness was soon filled with anger and a desire for retribution.

We don't live in a world that accepts an eye-for-an-eye type of punishment, but you can imagine this was something Sharon thought about on a daily basis. The next best result would be for the killer to be arrested and spend the rest of his life behind bars.

It looked like the family was going to get justice for Nikki when they were informed by the police toward the end of 1993 that her killer had been caught. His name was George Heron, and he was familiar to the family. He lived just around the corner from both Sharon and Nikki's granddad. Finally, the little girl would get a small sliver of justice, although things weren't as simple as that.

The evidence against Heron was compelling. He had a knife in his possession that matched Nikki's multitude of stab wounds. His worn-out shoes had drops of blood on them, as did his jacket. The man denied leaving the house the night Nikki vanished, but this was quickly found to be a lie when his sister admitted he'd been out that evening.

Not only that, she said, when her sibling returned home, he raced straight past her to the bathroom, where he locked himself in for half an hour. He gave himself a thorough wash and also tried to scrub his clothing clean. This was unusual behavior from Heron, according to his sister. She was suspicious of him that evening, so when it was found something had happened to a child that same night, her gut instinct caused her to turn her brother in.

Then there was the number of witnesses who saw Heron at his local pub that night. Along with a few pints of beer, the man bought some cheese and onion crisps to take away. *Why not eat them at the pub*, police asked Heron. *Was it because you used the lure of the crisps* - Nikki's favorite - *to entice the girl into the abandoned building*?

The interrogation Heron endured after his arrest isn't something the police would get away with today in most places. It was rough, filled with table banging and intimidation. Eventually, the man confessed to Nikki's murder.

At the trial, however, these heavy-handed tactics came back to haunt the investigators. It collapsed the case and sent George Heron free. After listening to the taped interrogation, there was no chance they could accept his admission of guilt as genuine. After all, he'd denied Nikki's murder over a hundred times until he couldn't take any more of the interrogation. He was broken and felt the only way out was to take the blame.

Of course, this didn't appease Nikki's family or the local community, who were baying for blood. The evidence against Heron was just too convincing for them to believe he wasn't the little girl's killer. They wouldn't accept him back into the community - he certainly wouldn't have an easy life; they would make sure of that. So, he was granted a new identity and was moved out of the area for his own safety.

Sharon couldn't let it lie - everybody knew Heron was the killer, and he'd gotten away with it. She wouldn't stop seeking justice, and in 1994, the year after Heron's trial, she embarked on a civil case against the man she believed killed her daughter. The charge against him was the beating of Nikki, which caused her death. Sharon won the case against Heron, who was ordered to hand over £7,000 in damages to the mother. However, Heron took off after hearing and couldn't be found. The police couldn't locate him, nor could Sharon or any would-be vigilantes. The money was never paid.

For two more decades, Sharon lived with the thoughts that her child's killer got away with murder, escaping all forms of justice by being handed a new identity and a fresh start. However, by now, she began to wonder if - even if the chance was small - that Heron really was Nikki's killer. These feelings of doubt were further compounded when, in 2016, a woman contacted Sharon out of the blue. The woman said she'd been babysitting the night Nikki was killed and may have seen something that could help the case move forward.

Nikki had been spotted that October evening, skipping behind a man, heading toward the direction of the Quayside Old Exchange.

The case was still cold, but it gave the police a nudge to reinvestigate the murder. It also gave Sharon a renewed fight to bring her daughter's killer to justice, and she began a petition to help convince the authorities to take a fresh look at the case. By 2017, a year later, Northumbria Police insisted they were still determined to snare the killer and brought new hope in making this a reality when they said they were conducting tests on DNA recovered from the scene.

Still, another agonizing year would pass, and the needle hadn't moved. Sharon had to consider the idea that she'd never get Nikki justice in her lifetime.

However, in April of 2018, a house raid in Stockton, about 40 minutes from Sunderland, brought a new suspect into the light - David Thomas Boyd. Where the evidence in Heron's case was compelling, more so was the evidence against Boyd. The 51-year-old denied any involvement, and it took authorities almost four years to charge the man, which they did in 2022.

Boyd stood trial in the spring of 2023, over 30 years after Nikki's murder.

The prosecution had a stack of damning evidence to present to the jury to help bolster their theory. They said Boyd had lured Nikki into the derelict building and got her to the basement, where he rained blows on her head from a brick. The child's skull was shattered from this attack, which rendered her unconscious. Afterward, he pulled out his knife and began stabbing the girl. For her to have been conscious while this was happening is a devastating thought, so it's a small mercy that she likely had no idea this awful knife attack was happening.

The attack was brutal and sustained. The little girl's vital organs were all pierced. The aggression and violence inflicted on the young girl was extreme.

Around 10 pm that night, a witness heard a scream coming from the area of the Old Exchange building. The time of this scream matched the recorded time of death forensics gave the girl.

The main piece of evidence that tied Boyd to the murder was the fact his DNA was found on the little girl's clothes. He surely couldn't explain this away - but he sure tried.

Boyd suggested that Nikki had his DNA on her because she'd somehow put her hands in his saliva after he'd been spitting from the height of his balcony. Once she'd smeared her hands in his spit, she then wiped it on her clothing. Or, perhaps he even accidentally spat directly on the girl as she walked past - he couldn't be sure.

This tale, if nothing else, made Boyd look like he was scrambling to rid himself of something he was certainly guilty of.

The prosecution also told the court how Boyd knew the layout of the abandoned building since he frequented there, luring young children to go "look for pigeons" with him. A strange thing for a 25-year-old to want to do, although not illegal. The fact he tried to entice random young children to do this with him was the worrying part.

Then there were the prior convictions Boyd had for assaulting young girls. A picture was developing as to what kind of man Boyd was, and it didn't show him in a good light at all. He'd also been arrested in the late 80s for bothering a group of children, which saw him grabbing a young girl before being detained by the police. Despite Boyd's refusal to admit to his guilt, he wouldn't take the stand to give evidence.

In May 2023, three decades after little Nikki Allan was killed, David Thomas Boyd was found guilty of her murder. He was given 29 years in jail before he could apply for parole, by which time Boyd would be in his mid-eighties.

This resulted in Northumbria Police issuing an apology to George Heron, who'd been made to leave the area and change his identity after being wrongfully accused of Nikki's murder.

Sharon Henderson is relieved her daughter's killer is finally behind bars, but she can't get rid of the sourness she feels about justice taking so long. She also felt the press coverage at the time painted her in a bad light: as a single mother who possibly neglected her little girl. As we know now, 90s press coverage was much less sympathetic than it is now. Headlines were tinged with blame towards the mother - not the man who'd killed the child, but rather the mother who was doing her best to take care of her young child.

This added to Sharon's PTSD, and she feels the past three decades have been a form of torture for her. Hopefully, the mother manages to find peace as time goes on and finds comfort in the knowledge that her little girl got a little justice in the end.

Final Thoughts

Thank you for taking the time to read Volume Five of the *Unbelievable Crimes* series. There have been some awfully gruesome cases covered in this anthology, another sobering reminder of what human beings are capable of. Just when you think you've heard of just about every crime committed, you learn of a wicked story that you've never come across before.

We'll never get to learn about every horrific crime committed, although as true crime enthusiasts, we sure know more than the average person about the horrors of the world. Sometimes, I'll stumble across a story that affects me, and I'll read as much as I can about it. Often, these crimes happened in other countries, and facts on the case are hard to come by. I will translate court documents (if there are any), go deep into various search engines, and reach out to people on social media to see if they can point me in the right direction for information. Frequently, I hit a dead end.

These crimes are filled with torture, human barbarity, and the worst kinds of assaults you can think of, but I'm restricted by the information made available by the country in which the crime took place. Sometimes, it's developing nations where I happen across a truly sickening crime and then hit a brick wall when trying to find more details about it. Their reporting of and dealing with such crimes can make piecing things together difficult. The internet certainly makes it easier to research a case, but it doesn't give a holistic view of the crime, making it tough for me to write about it.

All of this to say, there's so much we don't know, so many crimes that don't get reported, too many victims who never get the remembrance they deserve. It's a frustrating aspect of following true crime and a big reason why I try to cover crimes the majority of people haven't heard of.

In *Volume Six*, I continue this theme. By the time you're reading this, it should be available, or if not, it's not far away!

I've also taken on a new project: *Infamous Cults*. It's part of a new series I'm embarking on called *Infamous Crimes*. Each book in the series will focus on one specific category of crime. The first book, as you've already guessed, is dedicated to cults. I'll cover the leaders, the followers, and the shocking crimes of select cults. It's a slight shift from the *Unbelievable Crimes* series, but I'll continue to release publications in this series, too - after all, I have a lengthy list of crimes I want to cover.

With that in mind, I'd like to ask you what you'd like to see more of in this series. What crimes would you like to see covered? Would you prefer longer chapters or entire books dedicated to one singular crime? Are the books lengthy enough for you? Or are you happy with the way these anthologies are presented to you? What do you like about these books or my style of writing?

If you take the time to leave a review - something I'm always grateful for - feedback can be left here. Alternatively, the link to my upcoming newsletter is below. I'm looking to launch that in 2024 and connect with you all.

As always, I truly appreciate your readership, and I'll see you in the next one!

Take care,

Daniela

> Join the upcoming newsletter here:
>
> [Danielaairlie.carrd.co](http://danielaairlie.carrd.co)[1]

---

1. http://danielaairlie.carrd.co

www.ingramcontent.com/pod-product-compliance
Lightning Source LLC
Chambersburg PA
CBHW050256120526
44590CB00016B/2368